The QUINCY Miracle

A Rescue Never to be Forgotten

History of the Saints

SUSAN EASTON BLACK
Contributing Editors:
Glenn Rawson And Dennis Lyman

Cover images: top: *Refugees on the Mississippi*, by Julie Rogers; bottom: *Braving the Ice*, by A. D. Shaw.
Back cover: *Night Crossing*, by Liz Lemon Swindle.

Published by History of the Saints Inc.
Sandy, Utah

Cover and interior design by Susan Lofgren and Anna Oldroyd.
Editorial assistance by Bryant Bush; image research and cover design assistance by Adam Lyman.

Copyright © 2016 History of the Saints, Dennis C. Lyman, Glenn Rawson, Susan Easton Black, Jeffrey N. Walker, Gordon A. Madsen, William G. Hartley, Alexander L. Baugh, Richard E. Bennett, Lachlan Mackay, Reg Ankrom.

All rights reserved. No part of this book may be reproduced in any format or medium without the written permission of the publisher, History of the Saint's Inc. 1785 East Sunrise Park Drive, Sandy, Utah 84093

ISBN 978-0-9976694-0-4

Printed in China
First printing 2016

CONTENTS

Introduction 1
    by Glenn Rawson

The Aftermath: *Abusing Missouri Law* 9
    by Jeffrey N. Walker and Gordon A. Madsen

Missouri's 1838 Extermination Order and
the Mormons' Forced Removal to Illinois 35
    by William G. Hartley

Change of Venue: *The Gallatin Hearing and
the Escape of Joseph Smith and the Mormon
Prisoners from Missouri, April 1839* 59
    by Alexander L. Baugh

Quincy—*City of Refuge* 93
    by Susan Easton Black

Quincy, *the Home of Our Adoption* 113
    by Richard E. Bennett

In Golden Letters of Love: *The Kindness
of the Citizens of Quincy* 137
    by Lachlan Mackay

John Wood and the Mormons 151
    by Reg Ankrom

To the Citizens of Quincy 167
    by Eliza R. Snow

Grateful for the Kindness 171

In the winter of 1838–39, an extermination order issued by the governor of Missouri forced Latter-day Saints from the state.

Refugees on the Mississippi by Julie Rogers

INTRODUCTION

The Mormons were a people in trouble!

October 27, 1838, Missouri governor Lilburn W. Boggs signed Executive Order 44, declaring, "The Mormons must be treated as enemies, and must be exterminated or driven from the state if necessary for the public peace."[1] Thousands of Missouri militia forces were called out; they surrounded the Latter-day Saint settlement of Far West and demanded that the Mormons leave the state according to the governor's order.

But where could more than ten thousand people go on a moment's notice as winter approached? They were already on the western frontier of the United States. They couldn't go south; that would take them deeper into Missouri. They couldn't go west; that was Indian Territory. They couldn't go north; that was Iowa Territory, which was sparsely settled at best. The shortest and most direct route out of Missouri was due east across the Mississippi River and into Illinois. Based on an inviting word from a few Mormons already living in Quincy, Illinois, it was decided that the main body of the Latter-day Saints would go to Quincy to join the handful already there.

To hasten the Mormons' departure, mobs continued to prey on them, plundering, pillaging, raping, and burning. Joseph and Hyrum Smith were taken prison along with other Church leaders, and it was announced that they would be held until every Mormon had left the state. Joseph Holbrook commented, "We found that there was no more peace or safety for the saints in the state of Missouri. If the Church would make haste and move as fast as possible, it would aid much to relieve our brethren who are now in jail as our enemies were determined to hold them as hostages until the Church left the state. Every exertion was made in the dead of winter to remove as fast as possible."[2]

The flight of ill-prepared Mormons from the state of Missouri to Quincy, Illinois, is a saga of grand proportions. Their "Trail of Tears" was marked by bloodstained footprints.

Bloody Footprints
by Kelly Donovon

By December 1838, the Mormons began to move with whatever conveyance they could obtain, leaving behind much of what they owned. Brigham Young invited the Mormon brethren to covenant to assist the poor in leaving the state, and he did his best to gather resources to help them get out. He would not rest until all were safely out of Missouri.

By the bitter cold of January 1839, there were hundreds of men, women, and children strung along a two-hundred-mile trail leading east. It was the Latter-day Saint' "Trail of Tears." The weather was forbidding. At times the snow fell as much as a foot deep, accompanied by wind and bitter cold. At other times their way was marred by rain and deep mud. None had adequate food or clothing. Some were barefoot—their way across the prairie was marked by bloody footprints. Not all would survive the flight from Missouri.

By February, hundreds of Mormon refugees lined the west bank of the Mississippi River. Wagons filled with families and all they owned would pull to the river's edge, drop their human cargo and their meager belongings in the snow, and then turn back to help evacuate more of their fellow Saints.

At times the mighty river was impassable, as large chunks of floating ice prevented boat traffic on the river. Under these conditions, the Mormons were trapped: ahead was the impenetrable river, and behind were the Missourians, terrorizing them at every turn. Their only option was to hunker down and wait for the river to freeze so that they could cross over to Illinois on the ice.

Meanwhile, from across the river, citizens of Quincy saw firsthand the miserable drama of human suffering. The *Quincy Whig* documented that "A large number of families

are encamped on the opposite bank of the Mississippi waiting for an opportunity to cross. . . . If they have been thrown upon our shores destitute, through the oppressive people of Missouri, common humanity must oblige us to aid and relieve them all in our power."[3]

Sometimes the shelter for the refugees consisted of nothing more than a blanket thrown over a low-hanging limb. It was under these conditions that one Latter-day Saint woman, Martha Thomas, gave birth in a bed comprised of a rope contraption under quilts hung over a tree. Notwithstanding the risk, a delegation of Quincy residents braved their way across the river, bringing blankets and supplies. When they inquired of the Mormons what they needed, they were told: "If we should say what our present wants are, it would be beyond all calculation, as we have been robbed of our corn, wheat, horses, cattle, hogs, wearing apparel, houses and homes, and indeed of all that renders life tolerable. . . . Give us employment. Rent us farms. And allow us the protection and privileges of other citizens."[4]

Citizens of Quincy braved the dangerous, icy waters of the Mississippi to take food and supplies to Mormon exiles huddled together on the west bank of the river.

Braving the Ice by A. D. Shaw

In 1839, John Wood, the founder and mayor of Quincy, asked his community to give benevolent compassion to the Mormon refugees.

The river alternately froze and thawed throughout January and February. In late February 1839, the temperature dropped and the river froze solid. The Mormons braved the ice and came across. Eleven-year-old Mosiah Hancock talked of struggling to walk across the clear and slippery ice barefoot. As he neared the eastern bank the ice began to break up. "Father said, 'Run Mosiah!' and I did run," the boy remembered. "We all just made it on the opposite bank when the ice started to snap and pile up in great heaps and the water broke through."[5]

The relief of Mormons at finally being free of the terrors of Missouri was so great that some dropped to their knees on Quincy's shores and offered prayers of thanksgiving; others kissed the ground. Some made camp there on the banks of the river; others struggled up the bluffs to Washington Park, the main square of Quincy, where they set up makeshift tents. Wilford Woodruff described what he saw: "I saw a great many of the saints, old and young, lying in the mud and water, in a rainstorm, without tent or covering. . . . The sight filled my eyes with tears."[6]

The citizens of Quincy had compassion on the beleaguered Saints, especially the suffering women and children, and determined to take them in. The cry for compassion was led by Quincy's mayor and founder, John Wood. Orville Browning, another of Quincy's leading sons and an eyewitness of the Saints' suffering, declared, "Great God! Have I not seen it? Yes, my eyes have beheld the blood stained traces of innocent women and children in the drear winter, who had traveled hundreds of miles barefoot through frost and snow, to seek refuge from their savage pursuers."[7]

Compassion overwhelmed the people of Quincy, and as they had done before and would do again, they took in the homeless and ministered to the suffering. They brought the Mormons into their homes, shops, and even their barns. Every space that could be made hospitable was opened to the Mormons. The Mormons filled Quincy to overflowing before spreading out into other communities in Adams County. John Lowe Butler described the kindness that so typified the people of Quincy:

The old gentleman came to me and told me to bring my family up to one of his houses and we could live in it until we had been there a little while so that we should have a little time to look about us and get a place. . . . He never charged us anything for what we had. There were three or four other families living close to us that were Mormons. They were living in his houses that were joining ours. He treated them all with kindness. It seemed a new thing to us to be treated with so much kindness.[8]

Ezra T. Benson was one of the residents of Quincy who aided the Mormon refugees. When the Latter-day Saints moved north to Commerce, Ezra joined them.

The small community of Quincy, numbering fewer than two thousand people, somehow absorbed more than five thousand Mormons, giving them not only shelter but food, clothing, and jobs. When the Quincy citizens couldn't provide from their own stores, they sent out pleas for assistance as far away as Washington, D.C.

The Mormons would never forget what was done and by whom. A statement by the First Presidency proclaimed, "It would be impossible to enumerate all those who in our time of deep distress, nobly came forward to our relief and like the Good Samaritan poured oil into our wounds and contributed liberally to our necessities."[9]

In April 1839, the Mormon Prophet Joseph Smith escaped prison in Missouri and found his way to Quincy and his family.

For the brief period of three months, Quincy, Illinois, was the headquarters of Mormonism. Some citizens of Quincy—Ezra T. Benson among them—joined the Mormons and traveled on with them. Some of the Saints would travel no further and stayed among the good people of Quincy. Brigham Young's father, John Young, lies buried in Quincy.

By May 1839, Joseph Smith had moved fifty miles north of Quincy to Commerce, where he began building the foundations of a new city that would later be called Nauvoo. All but a handful of the Mormons left Quincy and settled in Nauvoo and other small settlements in Hancock County.

In the spring of 1839, Quincy boasted a population of about 1,600 residents. Although their numbers were few, they willingly assisted more than 5,000 Mormon refugees from Missouri. Their kindness and generosity is one of the greatest acts of humanitarian compassion ever demonstrated on American soil.)

Quincy, Illinois, circa 1840
by Kirt Harmon

But the miracle didn't stop with the initial rescue. Seven years later, in the fall of 1846, when the Mormons left Illinois for a new home in the Rocky Mountains, it was the citizens of Quincy who rallied. They loaded barges with food, clothing, and supplies, sailing the Saints up-river to aid the poorest of the Mormons in their exodus to the West.

The legacy of Quincy will endure forever as one of great humanitarian compassion. The deeds of Quincy's citizenry will live forever in the hearts of many who descended from those Mormons sheltered and saved in Quincy in 1839. Joseph Smith himself summed up the deeds of Quincy and their place in history: "They burst the chains of slavery and proclaimed us forever free! Quincy, our first noble city of refuge when we came from the slaughter in Missouri and with our garments stained with blood, should not be forgotten."[10]

— Glenn Rawson

History of the Saints

ENDNOTES

1. Lilburn W. Boggs to John B. Clark, October 27, 1838, *Document Containing the Correspondence, Orders, &c. in Relation to the Disturbances with the Mormons: And the Evidence Given Before the Hon. Austin A. King, Judge of the Fifth Judicial Circuit of the State of Missouri, at the court-House in Richmond, in a Criminal Court of Inquiry, Begun November 12, 1838, on the Trial of Joseph Smith, Jr., and Others, for High Treason and Other Crimes Against the State* (Missouri: *Boone's Lick Democrat*, 1841), 61.

2. Pamela Call Johnson, *Joseph Holbrook, Mormon Pioneer, Journal: With Commentary on the Winter He Spent with the Ponca Indians* (Bloomington, Indiana: AuthorHouse, 2013), 46.

3. *Quincy Whig*, March 1839.

4. Elias Higbee quote, in Joseph Smith, *History of the Church of Jesus Christ of Latter-day Saints*, ed. B. H. Roberts (Salt Lake City: Deseret Book, 1976 reprint), 3:269–70.

5. Mosiah Hancock, Autobiography, 17, L. Tom Perry Special Collections, Harold B. Lee Library, Brigham Young University, Provo, Utah.

6. "Wilford Woodruff History, from His Own Pen" *Millennial Star*, May 20, 1865, 311.

7. *History of the Church*, 4:368.

8. John L. Butler, "A History of the Biography of John L. Butler," L. Tom Perry Special Collections, 27–28.

9. First Presidency, "Proclamation to the Saints Scattered Abroad, January 15, 1841," in *History of the Church*, 4:267.

10. *History of the Church*, 4:292.

The Missouri state militia forced the surrender of Latter-day Saints at Far West on October 31, 1838, as well as the imprisonment of the Prophet Joseph Smith and several Church leaders.

The Extermination of the Latter Day Saints from the State of Missouri in the Fall of 1838 by H. R. Robinson

THE AFTERMATH
Abusing Missouri Law

by Jeffrey N. Walker and
Gordon A. Madsen

The surrender at Far West on October 31, 1838, marked the end of the Mormon conflict of 1838. It also marked the beginning of Joseph Smith's and some of his closest allies' incarceration, which did not end until their release while en route to Columbia, Missouri, in April 1839. The legal legitimacy of their imprisonment still remains mostly unanswered today.

Outside of Gordon Madsen's seminal work in 2004, "Joseph Smith and the Missouri Court of Inquiry: Austin King's Quest for Hostages,"[1] few have even attempted to explore the legality of the actions of the Missouri courts: Joseph Smith taken prisoner outside Far West, his preliminary hearing before Judge Austin A. King, the denial of his writs of *habeas corpus* while imprisoned in Liberty Jail, the grand-jury events in Gallatin, or the change of venue to Boone County that led to his release. This chapter addresses, albeit in general terms, each of these matters. In addition, this chapter will also look at what motivated the actions of military, political, and judicial officials involved in these events.

On this quiet, lonely ground overlooking the Grand River in Northern Missouri, the Missouri state militia forced thousands of Latter-day Saints to abandon their property in 1838.

By October 29, 1838, under the command of Major General Samuel D. Lucas, more than two thousand local militia troops gathered just south of Far West, preparing to make their final assault on the Mormons. Lucas's animosity toward the Mormons went back to 1833, when he was a central figure in driving the Mormons from Jackson County, where he lived. In an effort to find a peaceful resolution to the escalating conflict, Joseph Smith and other key leaders arranged through Colonel George M. Hinkle, the Mormon leader of the Caldwell County militia, to discuss terms of settlement with General Lucas. Relying on Hinkle's assurances that Lucas was prepared to discuss a peaceful surrender, Joseph Smith and his colleagues left Far West to meet with General Lucas.

When the Mormons arrived at Lucas's camp, Hinkle announced, "Here general are the prisoners I agreed to deliver to you."[2] Joseph Smith and the others—ultimately including Hyrum Smith, Sidney Ridgon, Lyman Wight, Parley P. Pratt, George Robinson, and Amasa Lyman—were taken prisoner. No legal process was used to validate taking any of these men into custody.

For Product Safety Concerns and Information,
please contact our EU representative GPSR@taylorandfrancis.com
Taylor & Francis Verlag GmbH, Kaufingerstraße 24,
80331 München, Germany

Printed by Integrated Books International,
United States of America

General Lucas's attempt that night to convict these civilians in a court martial, the only legal authority to which he had a claim, similarly lacked any legal efficacy. Brigadier General Alexander Doniphan, an attorney under Lucas's command, voiced his objection to Lucas's illegal death sentences for the men and refused to carry out the order. In response, Lucas backed down and left Far West with the prisoners, taking them to his hometown of Independence, Jackson County, and then to Liberty, Clay County.

This first step of incarcerating Joseph Smith and his companions was devoid of any legal process. Instead, complaints should have been filed in the local court naming each of the men and seeking arrest warrants against them.[3] If arrest warrants had been so issued by the court, Joseph Smith and the others would have known from the outset on what charges they were being arrested and incarcerated.[4] Instead, none of this occurred.

Lucas then brought the prisoners to Richmond, Ray County, where Fifth District Judge Austin A. King[5] was preparing to hear county prosecuting attorney Thomas Burch recite the charges that were to be brought against the prisoners by the state. As the Fifth Circuit judge, Austin King's jurisdiction included, in relevant part, Caldwell, Daviess, Ray, and Clay counties. Judge King should have recused himself from hearing the case and ordered it moved to a different circuit:[6] his impartiality was inescapably tainted by the death of his brother-in-law in 1833 while the Mormons were being driven from Jackson County.

Alexander W. Doniphan, a brigadier general in the Missouri militia, defied an order from his ranking officer, General Samuel D. Lucas, to execute Joseph Smith and fellow prisoners at the public square in Far West.

Circuit Judge Austin A. King presided over the legal hearings of Joseph Smith and fellow prisoners at Richmond, Missouri.

King's obvious bias was continually present during the hearing over which he presided. Lyman Wight, along with many others, recounted,

> I heard Judge King say on his bench, in the presence of hundreds of witnesses, that there was no law for the "Mormons," and they need not expect any. Said he, "If the Governor's exterminating order had been directed to me, I would have seen it fulfilled to the very letter ere this time."[7]

While held prisoner in Richmond, Missouri, Joseph Smith rebuked the guards for their foul language and their atrocities committed against Latter-day Saints.

Joseph rebuking the guards, Richmond Jail by Gary E. Smith

Upon arriving at Richmond, Joseph Smith and his fellow prisoners were jailed in a vacant home, where they were chained together to the center of the floor. They remained jailed in Richmond for three weeks. It was in this makeshift jail that Parley P. Pratt recorded the famous rebuking of the guards by Joseph Smith.

During this time, Major General John B. Clark (the overall militia commander) arrived in Far West, succeeding General Lucas, who had travelled with the prisoners to Richmond. General Clark conducted his own legally unauthorized interrogation of the Mormon citizens of Far West, determining that an additional forty-six men should be taken prisoner and forced to Richmond to be charged with various crimes before Judge King. Clark personally brought the additional prisoners to Richmond to appear before Judge King. Again, no complaint was filed in any court, nor was any arrest warrant issued—both of which were required by law.

The hearing before Judge King commenced on November 12, 1838, and lasted until November 29.[8] The hearing was formally referred to as a "court of inquiry," the equivalent of a preliminary hearing today. The purpose of the hearing was to determine whether there was sufficient evidence to establish "probable cause" that the prisoners had committed the alleged crimes.[9]

The record of this hearing is incomplete and was kept in such a manner that the Missouri legislature, which was tasked with reviewing the proceedings in December 1838, opined that "the evidence adduced in the examination there held, in a great degree ex parte [only one side's examination] and not of the character which should be desired for the basis of a fair and candid investigation."[10] The legal irregularities of the hearing were so pervasive that Hyrum Smith referred to the hearing as a "pretended court."[11] Alexander Doniphan, the lead attorney representing the Mormons, noted, "Though a legion of angels from the opening heavens should declare your innocence, the court and populace have decreed your destruction."[12]

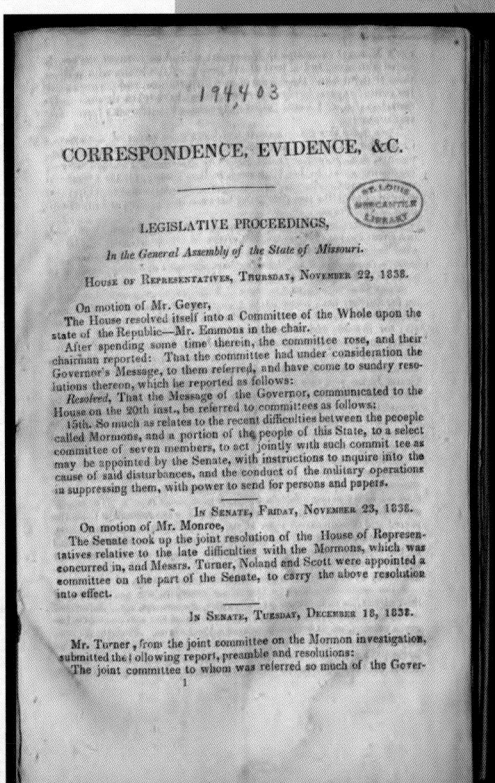

Court of Inquiry

These legal failings ranged from well-established due process errors to fundamental substantive legal mistakes. Consider the following summary of just a few of the legal errors committed during this preliminary hearing:

- No complaint based on sworn testimony was ever filed with a court describing the facts of a crime against any of the defendants.[13]
- No arrest warrants were issued by any court based on complaints and supporting sworn testimonies.[14]
- The defendants were held without even knowing the charges against them until the beginning of the hearing. Sidney Rigdon recorded, "No papers were read to us, no charges of any kind preferred, nor did we know against what we had to plead. Our crimes had yet to be found out."[15]
- All the defendants were tried together, despite the fact that different charges and corresponding different witnesses were necessary. Sidney Rigdon again recorded, "At the commencement we requested that we might be tried separately; but this was refused, and we were all put on our trial together."[16]

Judge King designated that Joseph Smith and five others were to be confined in Liberty Jail. Parley P. Pratt and four others were to remain in the Richmond Jail on charges of murder stemming from the October 1838 Battle of Crooked River.

Battle of Crooked River by C. C. A. Christensen

- Defendants were added throughout the hearing. The hearing started with fifty-three defendants (Joseph Smith and his six colleagues brought by General Lucas and forty-six prisoners brought by General Clark). Eleven additional defendants were added at different times throughout the hearing, bringing the total to sixty-four defendants. Two of the men were never even named as defendants who had been ordered by Judge King to appear before the grand jury, creating obvious due process failures.
- The record is incomplete regarding witness testimony. Sampson Avard was the star witness for the prosecution. As the former leader of the Danites, who led much of the opposition against the Missourians, he cut a deal with the state to avoid prosecution by implicating Joseph Smith and others. While his direct testimony is preserved in the official record, not a single cross-examination was recorded, despite the fact that those present recounted that he was vigorously cross-examined for more than a full day.[17]
- Witnesses for the defense were repeatedly intimidated, driven off, or named as defendants.[18] Ultimately, defense counsel told the defendants to stop naming or trying to bring witnesses, as it only put these people at substantial risk.

Joseph Smith was confined in Liberty Jail from December 1, 1838, to April 6, 1839.

- As the various alleged crimes were presented, there was no attempt to match the essential elements for the alleged crime with the witnesses or the defendants. In many cases, a review of the record reveals that the elements of alleged crimes were never established.[19]

In a case with so much procedure being out of order, it was not a surprise that Judge King ruled against the Mormons. Twenty-three of the defendants were bound over on charges ranging from arson,[20] burglary,[21] and robbery[22] to larceny.[23] As bail was available for each of these charges,[24] each man either provided cash for bail or pledged their property[25] with a bondsman. Ironically, these bondsmen were in most cases the very same people who had illegally arrested them in the first place.

Five of the men, including Parley P. Pratt, were charged with murder[26] in connection with the Crooked River Battle, in which three were killed: two Mormons (David Patten and Gideon Carter) and one Missourian (Moses Rowland). No Missourian was ever charged with the killing of the two Mormons. Bail was not available for this murder charge.[27] These six men were held in Richmond, since it was the county seat of Ray County, where the killings had taken place.

Finally, Joseph Smith and four others—Hyrum Smith, Alexander McRae, Caleb Baldwin, and Lyman Wight—were referred to the grand jury on the unique charge of treason, arising principally from the burning of two buildings in Daviess County. Sidney Ridgon was also charged with treason for two speeches he gave in Far West, Caldwell County. The propriety of the charges of treason were legally suspect from the outset, both as to whether the charge was available in

Memorial

> Farwest, Caldwell Co., Mo. Edward Partridge
> December 10th 1838   Heber C. Kimball
>   John   Taylor
>   Theodore Turly
>   Brigham Young
>   Isaac   Morley
>   George W. Harris
>   John   Murdock
>   John M. Burk
>
> A committee appointed by the citizens of the county, to draft this memorial and sign it in their behalf.
> Gen. Clarks speech to the ...

state court and whether the narrow basis for the charge was ever established on a *prima facie* basis.[28]

As with murder, bail was not available for the charge of treason.[29] Since there were no jails in either Daviess or Caldwell counties, where the alleged crimes occurred, Judge King ordered the prisoners to be held in the closest jail, which was in Liberty, Clay County. They arrived in Liberty under strong guard on December 1, 1838, to start what would be just more than a four-month winter incarceration.

Immediate efforts began to get the men released. The Missouri legislature was in session, and initial efforts aimed at seeking assistance from the legislature. On December 10, Brigham Young, Heber C. Kimball, John Taylor, and other leading Mormons drafted a lengthy "Memorial" to the legislature laying out the losses sustained by the Saints, starting with the "depravations" that occurred in Jackson County in 1833 and continuing through the wrongful incarceration of Joseph Smith and others in Liberty Jail.[30] Their report was countered by Governor Boggs's report to the legislature, which he submitted on December 5. The legislature formed a joint committee to investigate the matter on December 18. While the Mormons were initially hopeful for quick relief from the legislature (as the initial reports indicated that a speedy resolution was needed), these hopes were dashed when the joint committee recommended that no findings be made until after the grand jury was held in the spring of 1839. As justification for the delay, they cited fears that any findings by the legislature could unfairly impact the independence of the judiciary.

Joseph Smith and his co-prisoners wrote their own petition to the Missouri

Petitions for writ of *habeas corpus*

legislature dated January 24, 1839, focusing on the need for a fair hearing on the matter.[31] Smith explained the inherent prejudice that Judge Austin King had against them from the beginning of the court of inquiry:

> To the honorable Judge Thompkins or either of the Judges of the supream court for the state of Missouri.
>
> Your petitioners Alanson Ripley Heber C. Kimble, Joseph B. Noble, William Huntington, Joseph Smith jr beg leave respectfully to represent to your honor that Joseph Smith jr is now unlawfully confined and restrained of his liberty in Liberty jail Clay County (Mo) that he has been restrained of his liberty near five months your petitioners claim that the whole trans action which has been the cause of his confinement is unlawfull from the first to the last he was taken from his home by a fraude being practised upon him by a man by the name of George M. Hinkle and one or two others thereby your petitioner respectfully show that he was forced contrary to his wishes and without knowing the cause into the camp which was commanded by General Lucas of Jackson county and from thence to Ray county sleeping on the ground and suffering many insults and injuries and deprivations which were cal=culated in there nature to break down the spirits and constitution of the most robust and hardy of man-kind he was put in chains imediately on his being landed in Richmond and there under went a long and tedious exparte examination not only was it exparte but your petitioners can truly declair that it was a mock examination that there was not the least shaddow of honor or justice or law administered toward him but shear prejudice and the spirit of persecution and malice and prepossision against him on account of his religeon that the whole examinati[on] was an inquisatory examination your petitioners show that the said Joseph Smith jr was deprived of the privilege of being examined before the

> We the undersigned being [many of us] personally acquainted with the said Joseph Smith jr and the circumstances connected with his imprisonment do concur in the [petition &] testimony of the above named individuals, as most of the [transactions] therein mentioned we know from personal knowledge to be correctly set forth and from information of others believe the remainder to be true
>
> Amasa Lyman
> H G Sherwood
> James Newbury
> Cyrus Daniels
> Erastus Snow
> Elias Smith

> *But for the judge before whom the very men were to be tried for a capital offense to participate in an expression of condemnation of these same individuals, is to us, at least, apparently wrong; and we cannot think that we should, after such a course on the part of the judge, have the same chance of a fair and impartial trial as all admit we ought to have.*[32]

Joseph Smith received no reply.

Efforts were also directed at the courts seeking the release of Joseph Smith and the other prisoners. Petitions for writs of *habeas corpus* seeking a review of the Mormons' imprisonment were filed with local Clay County Judge Turnham.[33] The writ was granted and heard on January 25, 1839. Alexander Doniphan had recruited Peter Burnett to assist in representing the prisoners. Joseph Smith recorded that they "collected [their] witnesses the second time"[34] (the first being the King hearing), and Sidney Rigdon added that all of the written evidence was "read before the court."[35] At the end of the hearing, Judge Turnham released Rigdon because, as Peter Burnett recalled, "there was no sufficient proof in the record of the evidence before Judge

> In April 1839, Joseph Smith and fellow prisoners were transported to Gallatin, Missouri, for a grand jury hearing. Three members of the Grand Jury empaneled to hear the charges against Joseph Smith and fellow prisoners were among the mob/militia who participated in the Hawn's Mill Massacre.

King."[36] This is in accord with the law that speech alone was never sufficient to constitute treason. But Joseph Smith and the others were denied release and were recommitted to Liberty Jail. Clearly the incomplete nature of the record, especially the lack of any cross-examination of the prosecutors' star witness, Sampson Avard, made any credible review impossible.

The last effort in the courts for the release of the Liberty prisoners came on March 15, 1839, when Joseph Smith and the other prisoners sought relief from the Missouri Supreme Court, asking the court to look into the actual merits of the arrest and charges against them. This petition even included supporting affidavits from fellow Saints. Neither Joseph Smith nor the other prisoners ever received a reply.

With the spring term of the Court of Common Pleas for Daviess County set to commence on April 9, 1839, the five prisoners were moved from Liberty Jail in Clay County to Gallatin in Daviess County; they arrived on April 8. The Fifth Circuit had been split in January 1839, and Davies and Caldwell counties had been placed in the newly created Eleventh Circuit. The judge over this newly designated circuit was none other than Thomas Burch, the prosecuting attorney in the preliminary hearing before Judge King. A more obvious conflict of interest cannot be imagined. However, despite this conflict, Judge Burch empaneled the grand jury to hear the case against Joseph Smith and the other defendants charged with treason and other crimes.

The composition of the grand jury merits a brief mention. The central allegation against the Mormons in Daviess County was the burning and alleged robbery of Jacob Stolling's store in Gallatin and the burning of William Penniston's home outside Gallatin. The foreman of the grand jury was Robert P. Penniston Jr., William Penniston's brother. William Penniston's father, Robert Penniston Sr., was also called as a member of the grand jury. In addition, at least three members of the mob that participated in the Hawn's Mill Massacre—Nathaniel Blakley, John Brown, and Roger S. Rogers—sat on this grand jury. Clearly this was not an impartial jury as required by law.[37]

To make matters even worse, some of the grand jury members were called on at night to guard the prisoners.[38] Hyrum Smith recalled that these guards/jury members stayed up all night drinking and partying, causing a number of them to be literally incoherent when court was in session. Hyrum recalled that they "by-the-bye, were so drunk that they had to be carried out and into their rooms as though they were lifeless."[39]

While Judge King had taken nearly three weeks to conduct his preliminary hearing, Judge Burch took only days. Judge Burch did not need to hear all the evidence, as he had already concluded the guilt of the prisoners and other charged men who were out on bail, reportedly noting that the "Mormons ought to be hung without judge or jury."[40] The results were not unexpected: all the defendants were indicted on all crimes, including treason.

Grand Jury list

With the indictments handed down, defense counsel moved for a change in venue—a motion to move the case to a more neutral location in Missouri. Even though a newly enacted statute provided that a change in venue could be more easily procured based on affidavits by interested parties, Judge Burch denied the request.[41] However, Judge Burch on his own initiative ordered that the case be moved to Columbia, Boone County, on the basis of another statute that provided that a change in venue was mandated if the judge had "been counsel in the cause."[42] Such

The mere fact that members of the grand jury had participated in the massacre at Hawn's Mill just five months earlier suggests that this was not an impartial jury as required by law.

Hawn's Mill, Staging the Attack by Kelly Donovon

a change should have occurred prior to the case even being presented to the grand jury. However, with the indictments in place, Judge Burch belatedly moved the case, as he was required to do.

Such judicial manipulation is even more calculated when one examines the indictment pleadings themselves (especially those dealing with treason—the charge that kept Joseph

Some may say it gave people liberty to commit crimes against the Mormons. Clearly we can look at the court-martial of Joseph and his six colleagues the night of their arrest at Far West and the claimed authority of Boggs's order of extermination. Some may have claimed that the order provided them with extralegal powers. But the underlying purpose of the order was clearly to drive the Mormons from the state of Missouri. And I think the political method was to hold Joseph Smith and other key leaders—but principally Joseph—hostage until the Mormons were gone from the state. I believe the facts will indicate that, when looking at the totality, that such was Boggs's objective from the moment he gave the order on October 27 until it was orchestrated that Joseph and his colleagues were allowed to escape from their captors in April 1839." —*Jeffrey N. Walker*

Smith and five others incarcerated through the winter of 1838–39). Under Missouri's constitution, treason was established only if two independent witnesses testified about the same "overt act" of "levying war."[43] Every single one of the pleadings for the treason indictments have places for the "two witnesses" and the "overt acts" that were to be filled in as required by law. However, all of the pleadings delivered to the court in Columbia for treason were left blank as to both the witnesses and overt acts. No witnesses are identified, nor are any overt acts of levying war. Why did the judge or foreman of the grand jury leave these blank? Clearly the judge understood the law on treason that he prosecuted before Judge King. On what basis could a trial take place on these incomplete indictments?

The answer to these questions lies at the very center of why Joseph Smith was charged with treason in the first place. It appears clear, based on the records and accompanying testimony, that none of the people involved—Generals Clark or Lucas, Judge King, Governor Boggs, or Judge Burch—ever seriously contemplated actually trying Joseph Smith for treason.

Then why charge him with the crime? One most probable reason is straightforward: treason was one of only two crimes in Missouri for which bail was not available, meaning

The charge of treason is highly suspect in a state court. Nevertheless, Joseph Smith and fellow prisoners were charged with treason against the state of Missouri, a non-bailable offense.

that the defendant(s) must remain imprisoned at least until the grand jury was convened the following spring term. These military, political, and judicial men concertedly planned to hold Joseph Smith as a hostage on the charge of treason to make sure that the Mormons left the state of Missouri.

The plan worked. Through the winter of 1838–39, virtually all of the Saints made their way from Missouri to the eastern shore of the Mississippi River in Illinois instead of waiting for the original spring deadline. Consequently, by the time the grand jury indicted Smith there was no need—indeed no interest—in keeping Joseph Smith and his colleagues wrongfully imprisoned. Certainly, there was no interest in trying any of them for treason.

While it may be obvious from a legal perspective that no serious effort was being taken to try these men for treason, helping them out of the state was another matter. Following the faulty indictments, Judge Burch ordered that the prisoners be moved to Columbia, Boone County, Missouri, about a hundred miles southeast of Gallatin. Local sheriff William Morgan and four deputy sheriffs—William Bowman, John Brassfield, John Pope, and Wilson McKinney—were ordered

Evidence suggests that Joseph Smith was kept a prisoner/hostage in Liberty Jail to insure the Mormon exodus from the state of Missouri.

Joseph in Liberty Jail by Greg Olsen.

to move the prisoners. Judge Burch prepared a *mittimus* (essentially a transfer order), which Sheriff Morgan carried with him as he oversaw the moving of the prisoners.

However, the *mittimus* was curious in one material respect: Judge Burch had left blank the location where Sheriff Morgan was ordered to take the prisoners—Columbia, Boone County, Missouri, is never mentioned.[44] This was a most peculiar omission that allowed the sheriff to literally drop the prisoners off anywhere.

Sheriff Morgan and the rest of the party left on April 12, 1839, with the sheriff and deputies on horses and the five prisoners in the bed of a two-horse wagon. The party moved slowly toward Columbia. By April 16, four days later, they had covered fewer than thirty miles and were just entering Chariton County, Missouri. That night, the prisoners either escaped from the guards or were released by them.

> After Joseph Smith and his fellow prisoners were indicted on charges of treason, Judge Burch ordered a change of venue to Columbia, Missouri. It should be noted that a location is not specified on the *mittimus*.

For many scholars, history has clouded what happened the night of April 16, 1839. Joseph Smith never gave a full explanation. Lyman Wight, one of the prisoners, recounted that Sheriff Morgan told him that night that "he wished that to God that he was at home, and your friends and you also."[45] According to Hyrum Smith, Judge Burch told Sheriff Morgan never "to carry us [the prisoners] to Boone County."[46]

It appears that what ultimately happened that night was nothing more than the final step in a concerted conspiracy that started with the arrest of Joseph Smith and his imprisonment by Judge King. This understanding is founded on many accounts of the motives of these military, political, and judicial men and those under their control. Consider the blacksmith who was ordered by Judge King to chain Joseph Smith and others to the center of the makeshift jail in a vacant home in Richmond in November 1838, a man who told Hyrum and others that "the Judge [King] declared his intent to keep us in jail until all the 'Mormons' were driven out of the state."[47] Consider also the explanation given by Judge Turnham, the Clay County judge who heard Smith's and the others' writ of *habeas corpus* in January 1839:

> He said it was damned hard to be confined under such circumstances, for he knew we were innocent men; and he said **the people also knew it;** and that it was only a persecution, and treachery, and the scenes of Jackson county acted over again, for fear that we should become too numerous in that

upper country. He said that the plan was concocted from the governor down to the lowest judge and that damned Baptist priest, Riley, who was riding into town every day to watch the people, stirring up the minds of the people against us, for fear they would let us go.[48] [emphasis in original.]

Or consider the jailer at Liberty Jail who provided the following additional information:

> The jailer, Samuel Tillery, Esq., told us also that the whole plan was concocted by the governor down to the lowest judge in that upper country early in the previous spring, and that the plan was more fully carried out at the time that General Atchison went down to Jefferson city with Generals Wilson, Lucas, and Gillium, the self-styled Delaware Chief. This was sometime in the month of September, when the mob were collected at De Witt, in Carroll county. He also told us that the governor was now ashamed enough of the whole transaction, and would be glad to set us at liberty, if he dared do it. "But," said he, "you need not be concerned, for the governor has laid a plan for your release." He also said that Squire Birch [Burch], the state's attorney, was appointed to be circuit judge on the circuit passing through Daviess county, and that he (Birch) was instructed to fix the papers, so that we should be sure to be clear from any incumbrance in a very short time.[49]

This explanation is further corroborated by Emma Smith, who recorded that during her last visit to Liberty Jail on January 21, 1839, Sheriff Samuel Hadley told her, "All the authorities are waiting for is for you to get out of the state . . . [and] the prisoners will be let out . . . There is no reason for detaining them other than the unreasonable orders given."[50]

Such knowledge appeared to be well known to the Saints themselves, who left Missouri during the winter of 1838–39.

Emma Smith reported that her husband, Joseph Smith, was being held prisoner/hostage in Liberty Jail until the Mormons fled from the state of Missouri.

Take, for example, Daniel S. Thomas, one of the original forty-six prisoners taken by General Clark to Richmond. He recounted, "Word was received from Br. Joseph that there would be no chance for his deliverance until we were all out of the state."⁵¹ Joseph Holbrook, who was at the Battle of Crooked River, explained:

> *We found that there was no more peace or safety for the Saints in the state of Missouri. If the Church would make haste and move as fast as possible it would do much to relieve our brethren who were now in jail as our enemies were determined to hold them as hostages until the Church left the state. Every exertion was made in the dead of winter to remove as fast as possible and for those whom they, our enemies, held the greatest spite, to let their families go without them.*⁵²

Emma Smith, by Julie Rogers

As the foregoing illustrates, the purpose of the incarceration of Joseph Smith and others having been fulfilled by April 1839, the issue was not whether to release Joseph Smith and his fellow prisoners, but rather how, where, and when to release them. The how, where, and when would take form on the edge of Chariton County, Missouri, as the five lawmen stopped for the night with the five prisoners. The plan was straightforward: as Sheriff Morgan explained to the prisoners, "I shall take a good drink of grog and go to bed, and you may do as you have a mind to."⁵³ The records recount that three of the deputies also drank heavily of the whisky procured by the prisoners, who even sweetened it with honey.⁵⁴

The last guard, Deputy John Brassfield, assisted with the four prisoners' departure. A minimum of two horses was necessary for the prisoners to make their way to join the body of the Saints in Illinois. The prisoners explained that they had traded the clothing they received from the Saints when they arrived in Gallatin to the grand jury for one horse. John Brassfield then took a promissory note from Joseph Smith for $150 for the other horse. That promissory note still exists.⁵⁵ With two horses and the rest of the guards asleep on whisky, as Hyrum Smith cleverly put it, "we took our change of venue for the state of Illinois."⁵⁶

That promissory note is certainly a smoking gun on the debate as to whether Joseph Smith and the other prisoners escaped or were released. Indeed, it even looks like a gun. But additional facts and documents further support the conclusion that Joseph and his companions were indeed released, as Sheriff Morgan had been instructed to do by Judge Burch and as the blank *mittimus* permitted.

First, if the prisoners had indeed escaped, why did Sheriff Morgan and his deputies not pursue them? Missouri law required that they do so. Missouri penal code provided that if prisoners being transferred escaped, the officer was authorized to form a posse in any county the prisoners escaped to in order catch them. Failure to do so subjected the lawmen to criminal penalties of as many as five years in jail.⁵⁷

Second, when Sheriff Morgan and the other lawmen

On the evening of April 16, 1839, near Chariton County, Missouri, Deputy John Brassfield accepted from Joseph Smith a promissory note of $150 for a horse. Joseph Smith and his fellow prisoners then "escaped."

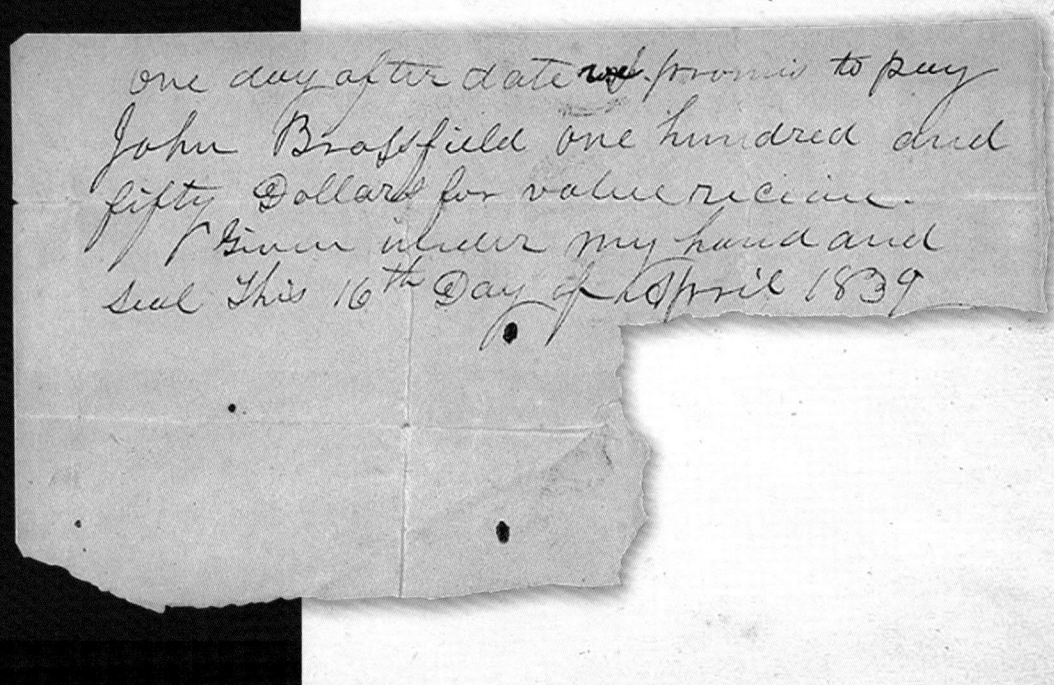

returned to Gallatin and the citizens learned that the prisoners had somehow escaped, as claimed by the officers, the citizens of Gallatin held a town meeting where they adopted a petition seeking the removal of Sheriff Morgan from office. The petition articulated just what the citizens of Gallatin believed happened:

Preamble

Whereas many reports are in circulation relative to the escape of the mormon prisoners, from the Sheriff of this County, on his way from here, to Columbia, where he was conveying them to gaol, which have created and confirmed the suspicion of this meeting that their escape was not accidental nor unavoidable; but on the contrary, from facts within our own knowledge and all the circumstances taken together we are forced to adopt the opinion that they were willfully set at liberty. Yet from the fact that the evidence upon which this meeting bases its opinion of the guilt of the Sheriff might not, in a court of law, be admitted, or not sufficient to convict them (the Sheriff & his guard) and thus subject them to that punishment they deserve, and that the law would inflict. Therefore an expression of opinion on this subject should be made publickly to the world, condemning and reprobating the conduct of the actors in this disgracefull affair and hold them up to the contempt of all good and honourable citizens. The most favourable construction that can posebly be put on this unfortunate affair is, that the Sheriff was guilty of a palpable and wilfull neglect of his official duty. In fact the whole tenor of his official conduct

> When citizens of Gallatin, Missouri, learned that the Mormon prisoners had escaped, they drafted a petition for the removal of Sheriff Morgan from office.

Whereas many reports are in circulation relative to the escape of the Mormon prisoners, from the Sheriff of this County, on his way from here to Columbia where he was conveying them to goal [jail], which created and confirm our suspicion of this meeting that their escape was not accidental or unavoidable; but on the contrary, from the facts within our knowledge and all the circumstances taken together we are forced to accept the opinion, that they were willfully set at liberty.[58]

Third, neither Sheriff Morgan nor any of the lawmen who served under him during the transfer of Joseph Smith and the other prisoners was brought before Judge Burch for dereliction of duty.

Finally, when the indictments did finally arrive in the Boone County courts, the cases were all continued until the August 1840 term, when the prosecuting attorney moved the court for their dismissal. Circuit Court Judge Thomas Reynolds granted this motion. Judge Reynolds became governor of Missouri in late 1840, after which he started his own attacks on Joseph Smith—but that is another story for another time.

Jeffrey N. Walker

Jeffrey N. Walker is the series manager and coeditor of the Legal and Business Records series of The Joseph Smith Papers, and is a member of the editorial board. He served as associate managing editor of the Papers until 2012. He completed a BS from Western Michigan University and a JD from the J. Reuben Clark Law School, Brigham Young University, where he was an editor for the Brigham Young University Law Review. He currently serves as adjunct professor at the J. Reuben Clark Law School. He has been in private practice since 1988 and has developed various businesses, including a manufacturing company and national watch company. He has written and spoken widely on Joseph Smith's legal affairs and is currently preparing a multivolume work on Oliver Cowdery's legal practice. He is a trustee and treasurer for the Mormon Historic Sites Foundation and the managing editor of *Mormon Historical Studies*.

Gordon A. Madsen

Gordon A. Madsen serves the Joseph Smith Papers as senior coeditor of the Legal and Business Records series. He received BS and JD degrees from the University of Utah. He served as Utah deputy district attorney from 1957 to 1959 and as assistant attorney general, 1959–1964. He has been in private practice since 1964. His civic and professional contributions include being a member, Constitutional Revision Commission; member, Judicial Qualifications Commission; member, Judicial Nominating Commission (Third Judicial District); chairman, Eminent Domain Section and Legislative Section of Utah State Bar; and member, Utah House of Representatives, 1969–1971. Among his publications are "State Police Power Held to Override Bankruptcy Act in Financial Responsibility Case," *Personal Finance Law Quarterly* 16.3 (Summer 1962): 97–100; "Joseph Smith's 1826 Trial: The Legal Setting," *BYU Studies* 30.2 (Spring 1990): 91–108; and "Joseph Smith and the Missouri Court of Inquiry," *BYU Studies* 43.4 (2004): 93–136.

ENDNOTES

1. Gordon Madsen, "Joseph Smith and the Missouri Court of Inquiry: Austin King's Quest for Hostages," *BYU Studies* 43, no. 4 (2004):93–136.

2. "Lyman Wight Sworn," *Times and Seasons*, July 15, 1843, 267.

3. An Act to Regulate Proceedings in Criminal Cases (Mar. 21, 1835), art. II, sec. 2, in *Revised Statutes of the State of Missouri*, 2nd ed. (St. Louis: Chambers, Knapp & Co, 1840), 474.

4. Act to Regulate Proceedings in Criminal Cases, sec. 3, 475.

5. Clearly, Judge King fully understood these and other statutory requirements, as he was the chairman of the committee organized by the Missouri legislature to compile and oversee the printing of the *Revised Statutes of the State of Missouri*. See *Revised Statutes*, 2.

6. Act to Regulate Proceedings in Criminal Cases, art. V, sec. 15, 486.

7. "Lyman Wight Sworn," 268.

8. An Act to Establish Judicial Districts and Circuits, and Prescribe the Times and Places of holding Courts (March 17, 1835), in *Revised Statutes*, sec. 21, 164. (The Fifth Circuit Court for Ray County commenced its November term on the first Monday in November, which was November 4, 1838).

9. A court of inquiry was predicated on a properly verified complaint and issued warrant. Act to Regulate Proceedings in Criminal Cases, art. II, secs. 2, 3, 12, and 13, 474–76. A finding of probable cause was similarly required by statute. Act to Regulate Proceedings in Criminal Cases, secs. 21 and 22, 476–77.

10. *Correspondence, Orders, &c. in Relation to the Disturbances with the Mormons; and the Evidence* (Fayette, MO: Missouri General Assembly, 1841), 2.

11. "Hyrum Smith Sworn," *Times and Seasons*, July 1, 1843, 254.

12. Parley P. Pratt, *Autobiography of Parley Parker Pratt* (New York: Russell Brothers, 1874), 233.

13. Act to Regulate Proceedings in Criminal Cases, art. II, sec. 2, 474.

14. Ibid.

15. "Sidney Rigdon Sworn," *Times and Seasons*, Aug. 1, 1843, 277. Lyman Wight similarly supported this failure. See "Lyman Wight Sworn," 268.

16. "Sidney Rigdon Sworn," 276. This was done in violation of the protections and procedures outlined in Act to Regulate Proceedings in Criminal Cases, art. II, secs. 13–19, 476.

17. Act to Regulate Proceedings of Criminal Cases, art. II, sec. 20, 476.

18. Rough Draft Notes of History of the Church, 1838–07 (Aza Judd, Jun.), Church History Library, Salt Lake City. This was done in violation of the provisions in Act to Regulate Proceedings in Criminal Cases, art. II, sec. 15, 476.

19. This was done in violation of the provisions of Act to Regulate Proceedings in Criminal Cases, art. II, secs. 21 and 22, 476–77.

20. As defined in An Act Concerning Crimes and Their Punishment (Mar. 20, 1835), art. III, secs. 1–12, 174–75, in *Revised Statutes*.

21. As defined in Act Concerning Crimes and Their Punishment, art. III, secs. 13–19, 175–76.

22. As defined in Act Concerning Crimes and Their Punishment, art. III, secs. 25–29, 177.

23. As defined in Act Concerning Crimes and Their Punishment, art. III, secs. 30–35, 177–78.

24. As defined in Act Concerning Crimes and Their Punishment, art. III, secs. 35 and 37, 478.

25 As provided for in Act Concerning Crimes and Their Punishment, art. III, sec. 26, 177.

26 As defined in Act Concerning Crimes and Their Punishment, art. I, secs. 1–3, pp. 167–68.

27 Constitution of the State of Missouri, art. XIII, sec. 11, in *Revised Statutes*, 28.

28 Constitution of the State of Missouri, art. XIII, sec. 15, 28.

29 Constitution of the State of Missouri, art. XIII, sec. 11, 28.

30 Rough Draft Notes of History of the Church, 1838–038.

31 Joseph Smith Letterbook, 2:66–67, Joseph Smith Collection, Church History Library.

32 Joseph Smith Letterbook, 2:67.

33 Act to Regulate Proceedings on Writs of *Habeas Corpus* (March 6, 1835), art. I, secs. 1–3, in *Revised Statutes*, 297–98.

34 Joseph Smith to Isaac Galland, March 22, 1839, Joseph Smith Collection, Church History Library.

35 "Sidney Rigdon Sworn," 277.

36 Peter Hardeman Burnett, *Recollections and Opinions of an Old Pioneer* (New York City: D. Appleton and Co., 1880), 53–55.

37 An Act Concerning Grand and Petit Jurors (March 7, 1835), sec. 15, in *Revised Statutes*, 343.

38 "Hyrum Smith Sworn," 254; Grand Jurors, sec. 15, 343, provides that officers of the court (here guards) cannot serve as jurors. As the records are sealed in grand jury proceedings, no record exists to determine whether Peter Burnett or Amos Reese, defendants' counsel, moved to remove any of these or other jurors for cause, as provided for in Act Concerning Grand and Petit Jurors, secs. 10 and 13, 343. What is clear is that the Pennistons and the three mobbers at Hawn's Mill remained on the grand jury that indicted Joseph Smith and fellow Mormons.

39 "Hyrum Smith Sworn," 254.

40 "Lyman Wight Sworn," 268.

41 Governor Boggs signed into law this new, more liberal statute of changing venue on February 13, 1839 (Missouri Senate Journal, 449). Stephen Markham carried this new legislation to Gallatin during the grand jury hearings.

42 Act to Regulate Proceedings in Criminal Cases, art. V, sec. 15, 486.

43 Constitution of the State of Missouri, art. XIII, sec. 15, 28.

44 "Lyman Wight Sworn," 269.

45 Ibid.

46 "Hyrum Smith Sworn," 256.

47 "Hyrum Smith Sworn," 254.

48 Ibid.

49 "Hyrum Smith Sworn," 254–55.

50 Linda K. Newell and Valeen T. Avery, *Mormon Enigma: Emma Hale Smith, Prophet's Wife, "Elect Lady," Polygamy Foe* (Urbana, IL: University of Illinois Press, 1994), 78.

51 Kate W. Kirkham, *Daniel Stillwell Family History* (Salt Lake City: Private Printing, 1927), 19.

52 "The Life of Joseph Holbrook, Written by His Own Hand," in *An Enduring Legacy*, 3 vols. (Salt Lake City: Daughters of the Utah Pioneers, 1978), 1:184.

53 Pratt, *Autobiography*, 242.

54 Ibid.

55 Promissory Note dated April 16, 1839, Joseph Smith Collection, Church History Library.

56 "Hyrum Smith Sworn," 256.

57 Act to Regulate Proceedings in Criminal Cases, art. III, sec. 38, 196.

58 Citizen Petition, Joseph Smith Collection, Church History Library.

Head Quarters of the Militia
City of Jefferson
Octr 27 1838

Sir
 Since the order of this morning to you directing you to cause 400 mounted men to be raised within your division I have received by Amos Rees Esqr of Ray & Wiley C. Williams Esqr one of my Aids information of the most appalling character which entirely changes the face of things and places the Mormons in the attitude of an open and avowed defiance of the laws and of having made war upon the people of this State. Your orders are therefore to hasten your operations with all possible speed. The Mormons must be treated as enemies and must be exterminated or driven from the State if necessary for the public peace. Their outrages are beyond all description. If you can increase your force you are authorized to do so to any extent you may consider necessary. I have just issued orders to Majr Genl Willock of Marion Co to raise 500 men and to march them to the Northern part of Daviess and there unite with Genl Doniphan of Clay who has been ordered with 500 men to proceed to the same point for the purpose of intercepting the retreat of the Mormons to the North. They have been directed to communicate with you by express, you can also communicate with them if you find it necessary. Instead therefore of proceeding as at first directed to reinstate the citizens of Daviess in their homes you will proceed immediately to Richmond and there operate against the Mormons. Brig Genl Parks of Ray has been ordered to have four hundred of his Brigade

Missouri Governor Lilburn W. Boggs's extermination order

Missouri's 1838
EXTERMINATION ORDER

and the Mormons' Forced Removal to Illinois

by William G. Hartley

On October 27, 1838, Missouri Governor Lilburn W. Boggs ordered that "the Mormons must be treated as enemies, and must be exterminated or driven from the state if necessary for the public peace."[1] That order is what caused seven thousand or more members of The Church of Jesus Christ of Latter-day Saints to leave homes, farms, and businesses in northwestern Missouri and seek refuge outside the state. Most of them left during winter in desperate conditions. On foot, on horseback, and with wagons, they trudged the width of Missouri to the Mississippi River and crossed into Quincy, Illinois, where they found temporary refuge.[2]

The "Mormon War" in Missouri

The Mormon troubles in upper Missouri are well documented and explained in several published histories.[3] In a nutshell, what is termed "the Mormon War" in Missouri annals broke out in the summer and fall of 1838, resulting in a variety of tragedies: shooting; burning of houses; pillaging of crops and livestock; a skirmish called the Battle of Crooked River on October 24, in which a handful lost their lives; and the Hawn's Mill Massacre on October 30, in which some seventeen innocent Mormons were brutally shot to death and fourteen others wounded by more than two hundred Missouri vigilantes.

Apparently the massacre at Hawn's Mill happened just before news of Governor Boggs's extermination order arrived.[4] By the month's end, some twenty-five hundred Missouri troops under Major General Samuel D. Lucas had marched to the Mormon headquarters of Far West. Lucas read the extermination order to Latter-day Saint negotiators and set terms for the Saints' surrender, which took place on November 1, 1838.[5]

Governor Boggs's order was a military order that was modified in the field but that technically lost its legal force when the military situation ended by December 1. Since the Mormon exodus took place from December to April, "civilians without any authority enforced an expulsion policy that did not originate with the governor in the first place."[6]

First Removals: Prisoners, Fugitives, and Daviess County Mormons

Armed with the governor's order, General Lucas imposed four terms on the conquered Mormons: take their leaders into custody; use their personal property to repay costs, debts, and damages Missourians suffered; confiscate all arms; and order the Mormons to leave the state.[7] When General John B. Clark of the Missouri state militia replaced General Lucas a few days later, he intended to enforce all of General Lucas's terms of capitulation. Instead, early snows and deprivations the Mormons were suffering "induced me to modify the terms," General Clark said, "and not require them to remove forthwith." He gave permission for them to remain "until their convenience suited them in the spring."[8]

Within a month of the Missouri army's arrival, three Mormon "removals" took place. First, when the troops arrived at

General Samuel D. Lucas commanded the militia troops that forced the surrender of Latter-day Saints at Far West.

Courtesy Bill Curtis

Far West, Latter-day Saint leaders instructed Mormon militiamen who had been involved in the Battle of Crooked River to flee for their lives. By November 1, dozens (and perhaps as many as a hundred) had fled. Most escaped northward into Iowa Territory, their journeys made harrowing by lack of proper clothing, equipment, and food. Second, General Lucas's soldiers arrested and marched about fifty men off to prisons approximately thirty miles south, including Church leaders Joseph Smith, Hyrum Smith, Sidney Rigdon, and Parley P. Pratt. Third, General Clark ordered all those living in neighboring Daviess County to leave that county. This was the fourth time Mormons had been forced from a Missouri county.

Accordingly, Daviess County Saints deserted their houses and crops in "very cold" weather. They left behind flocks and herds because the "mob had relieved them from the trouble of taking care of them, or the pain of seeing them starve to death—by stealing them." William Huntington calculated that the Saints in Daviess County alone lost 29,465 bushels of corn due to the military takeover.[9]

This 1907 George Edward Anderson photograph shows the approximate location of the Battle of Crooked River, a tragedy of the Mormon War of 1838. Latter-day Saints who participated in the battle were among the first Mormons to flee from Missouri in December 1838.

Through cold days and nights in November and December, the Latter-day Saints maintained a hope that they would not have to leave Missouri. But the state government declined to reverse the extermination order, so the Mormons had to face the reality of leaving by spring, which they hoped meant April. When the year 1839 opened, the extermination order still stood "because private regulators were still at the ready" in place of state militia. The order essentially "dignified forced removal by unauthorized civilians."[10]

Individual Departures

Given Church counsel to leave the "Land of Promise," many did so as soon as they could. Because it was so late in the year, those wanting to find housing and employment in urban centers had only two good options—St. Louis, Missouri, or Quincy, Illinois.

St. Louis, an "oasis of tolerance" for Mormons, drew those who could afford river-boat passage and those families who were physically unable to undertake two weeks of overland travel with wagons or on foot.[11] Many families went to Richmond and then took boats down the Missouri River to St. Louis. Others went to Quincy, two hundred miles directly east of Far West.[12]

Difficult Winter of Waiting

Those who did not or could not leave Missouri in November and December crowded together in Far West and nearby cluster settlements, sharing roofs, yards, outbuildings, clothing, and food. Hundreds of refugees stood in need of help because they had "been robbed of our corn, wheat, horses, cattle, cows, hogs, wearing apparel, houses and homes, and indeed, of all that renders life tolerable."[13] Newlywed Joseph Holbrook said that his wife "had very poor health" that fall and winter because of being exposed to "inclement weather by having to remove from place to place as our house had been burned and we were yet left to seek a home wherever our friends could accommodate us and for my safety." The Saints, "in flourishing condition but a few months before," he said, "were now destitute. I could

Latter-day Saints gathered in from outlying settlements to Far West. Many were in need of help, having been robbed of their possessions.

have commanded some two thousand dollars but now I had only 1 yoke of old oxen and 2 cows left."[14]

Far West became a refugee camp, one that lacked sufficient housing and food for all the homeless people forced to winter there. Many who were not homeless had lost property when the Missouri victors took their share of Mormon spoils in early November. On November 6, Brigham Young wrote that the troops at Far West plundered "bedding, clothing, money, wearing apparel, and everything of value they could lay their hands upon. . . . The soldiers shot down our oxen, cows, hogs, and fowls, at our own doors, taking part away, and leaving the rest to rot in the streets. The soldiers also turned their horses into our fields of corn."[15]

Heavy snow fell on November 7, 8, and 11. "It has been very cold for a month past," Albert Rockwood recorded on November 19. "The ground is and has been frozen several inches for a number of weeks. . . . Potatoes that are not dug have frozen solid."

Lucy Mack Smith wrote, "It was enough to make the heart ache to see the children, sick with colds, and crying around their mothers for food, whilst their parents were destitute of the means of making them comfortable."

Winter exposure took its toll. Among some seven thousand Saints staying in and near Far West. Tents, covered wagons off their wheels, and makeshift huts provided poor protection for many. Mary Ivers said that "for six months I never lodged in a house."[16] Lucy gathered refugees around her home in Far West. Lucy Mack Smith, the Prophet Joseph Smith's mother, allowed her yard to become a campground for the homeless:

> There was an acre of ground in front of our house, completely covered with beds, lying in the open sun, where families were compelled to sleep, exposed to all kinds of weather; these were the last who came into the city, and as the houses were all full, they could not find a shelter. It was enough to make the heart ache to see the children, sick with colds, and crying around their mothers for food, whilst their parents were destitute of the means of making them comfortable.[17]

Joseph C. Kingsbury said that families near him lodged in covered wagons and suffered greatly from freezing weather and the shortage of food in Far West.[18] James Carroll and his family lived in an open-frame structure. After nights when it snowed, he said, they sometimes awoke with their beds covered with snow.[19] By December, all but eleven of the Mormon prisoners were released and returned to help their families. Church leaders at Far West felt special obligations to help the families of the hundred or so fugitives and of those still in prison, including those of Joseph and Hyrum Smith, Sidney Rigdon, Lyman Wight, and Parley P. Pratt.[20]

Church Committee for Removal

The question of how so many people could move was of prime concern. By early January, Church authorities called and sent a number of men on missions throughout the United States to reassure members outside Missouri that the Church was still operating. The missionaries were also to solicit funds and help for the Missouri refugees.[21]

While most Latter-day Saints used their own resources to evacuate individually, many lacked wagons and teams and

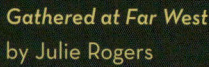
Gathered at Far West
by Julie Rogers

needed assistance. By mid-January, Brigham Young, the Church's senior authority in Far West, sought ways to help the needy. At public meetings held in late January, a Committee for Removal was appointed to supervise the evacuation and assist those needing help, and people were asked to pledge to leave no one behind.[22] In response, 380 men signed the covenant to

> *stand by and assist one another, to the utmost of our abilities, in removing from this state in compliance with the authority of the state; and we do hereby acknowledge ourselves firmly bound to the extent of all our available property, to be disposed of by a committee who shall be appointed for the purpose of providing means for the removing from this state of the poor and destitute who shall be considered worthy, till there shall not be one left who desires to remove from the state.*[23]

Brigham Young appointed a Committee for Removal to supervise the Mormon evacuation of Far West and to assist those in need.

An unresolved question was whether the Saints should scatter or go somewhere they could live together again. Albert Rockwell wrote on January 30, "It is thought by some we shall not gather again in large bodies at present, still we do not know[.] Our leader is gone, we have none to tell us what to do by direct Revelation."[24] Quincy, however, became the immediate destination, even if temporary, for those going overland.

The Committee on Removal, facing an "arduous task," visited among the Saints seeking money and promises of wagons and teams.[25] They collected donations of furniture, farm implements, and money from farm sales.[26] The committee decided to move the families of the prisoners first and as soon as possible. On February 6, Committeeman Markham initiated the Church-assisted removals by helping the Prophet's wife Emma, the children, and a couple by the name of Holmes. On February 15, "after a journey of almost insupportable hardships," Markham unloaded his passengers by the river opposite Quincy; he then and headed back to Far West for another load.[27]

From Far West the committee sent agents eastward to deposit corn for the Latter-day Saints to use along the way, to contract for ferries, and to ensure security

The shortage of wagons and teams made it impossible for the Mormons to flee as a group from Far West. Many a teamster transported a family to the Mississippi River and left them in the snow before returning to Far West to transport another.

Family in the Snow
by Julie Rogers

for the travelers.[28] The Committee directed appeals for help to the state government, the press, communities in and beyond Missouri, and Latter-day Saints outside Missouri. Missouri's legislature appropriated $2,000 to aid citizens in Daviess and Caldwell counties, including Mormons, but little real help reached the poor Saints.[29]

In 1839, John P. Greene, Brigham Young's brother-in-law, published a pamphlet designed to arouse national sympathy for the Saints' plight. Regarding the situation at the time of the exodus, he wrote:

> Many were stripped of clothing and bedding. Many sold all their household stuff to pay the immediate expenses of their journey. Many without cattle, horses, or waggons, had no means of conveyance. In this situation it was thought proper to make some general effort for the removal of the helpless families—a contribution was raised from among the Mormons who had means, and a committee appointed for its expenditure. It was through this charity among themselves that the destitute were enabled to remove to the state of Illinois.[30]

Seeking Quincy

In January and February, the flow of Saints traveling on their own using their own resources got under way. They started the exodus in winter for several reasons.[31] Some saw no reason to delay the inevitable and, having the ways and means to do so, left. A belief grew that Joseph Smith would not be released from prison until the Saints had left the state, so he would be helped by their migrating sooner than planned. Armed patrols were also threatening the Mormons in January, so in a public meeting on January 26, the people agreed to remove themselves immediately.

In early February, Far West experienced good weather, favorable for making the journey. By February, too, individuals were running out of food and supplies and needed to go elsewhere to meet their basic needs. Lastly, it would take time to move so many people, especially when many had to wait for wagons to return for them.

As early as January 10, Albert Rockwood left Far West in company with another family. They covered two hundred miles and reached the Mississippi River in twelve days. In February, Rockwood wrote that "most of the Church cross the River & come to this place [Quincy]. The people here receive us Quite Friendly & think of us as an abused people."[32]

An 1840 Missouri map shows two road networks the Latter-day Saints could follow east to Quincy. One route ran

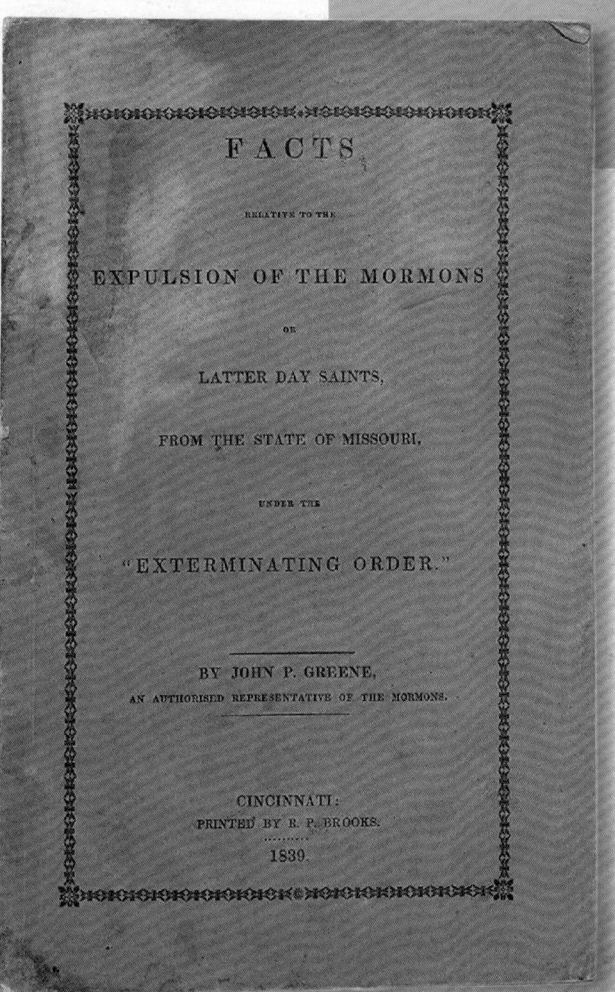

Facts Relative to the Expulsion by John P. Greene. The pamphlet of John P. Greene was intended to arouse the sympathies of the nation towards the plight of the Latter-day Saints.

east from Far West with an arch northward, passing south of Chillicothe, going through Macon and Shelbyville, making a bend south to Oakdale, and going back up to Palmyra. Palmyra, twenty miles southwest of Quincy, was the last town the refugees passed before crossing the South and North Fabius rivers to reach the Mississippi shoreline. Because that trans-Missouri route was not well settled, some preferred it so they could avoid trouble with locals. The Committee for Removal deposited food along that route to help the needy.

The second route was two dozen miles farther south and ran roughly parallel to the northern one—going from Tinney's Grove (twenty miles from Far West) to Keytesville, Huntsville, and Paris, then northwest to Palmyra and north to the Fabius River mud flats.[33]

Threats coupled with a surprise break in the weather spawned heavy traffic in February. However, once this new wave of refugees was on the road to Quincy, the weather worsened. On February 22, a man arriving at Far West from Illinois counted 220 eastbound wagons along his route. At the end of February, said the Daniel Stillwell Thomas family, more than 100 families were camped opposite Quincy. Mother Lucy Mack Smith obtained a wagon to haul her and three

Most Latter-day Saints made their way eastward across the Mississippi River to Quincy, Illinois.

The map suggests two roads the Latter-day Saints might have taken as they fled from Missouri in the winter of 1838–39.

other families' baggage, and they left on February 24. Rains turned the road to mud; then, six miles from the Mississippi, snow and hail fell, making the normally swampy river flats worse. Mother Smith's group waded six miles, camped without a tent, and by morning had six inches of snow covering their bedding.[34] Many, said George Washington Gill Averett, traveled "in Colde weather thinly clad and poorly furnished with provisions."[35]

Daniel Stillwell Thomas and his wife, Martha, left Far West on February 14 with one wagon and five children who had but one pair of shoes among them. Martha was eight months pregnant. The snow was six inches deep, Martha recalled. "To hear them [the children] crying at night with their feet cracked and bleeding was a grievous sight for a mother to bear. I would often grease them and put on clean stockings instead of making them wash [their feet] when going to bed."

The Thomas family stalled for two weeks at the river, giving up their wagon to bring others from Far West. Daniel rigged a tent out of forked stakes, poles, and quilts. "Our corn bread was frozen so hard I had to take the ax and break it and give it to the children to gnaw at, the bread looking like chunks of ice," Daniel said. When the river opened the family crossed in two boats. Martha and the four children waited on the Quincy side, but husband and son did not come by sunset. Martha wrapped the four small children in bedclothes, and

By late February 1839, hundreds of Mormon exiles traveled east toward Quincy under difficult winter conditions.

Exodus by Glen S. Hopkinson

they huddled together to endure the night. She said she cried that night for the first time during the exodus. The family reunited the next day and moved into town. A few days later

This is the story of Daniel Stillwell Thomas and his wife, Martha. They are crossing the river in February. They have a wagon and a pair of steers, five children, and one pair of shoes among them. The first twenty miles the snow is six inches deep and Martha is eight months pregnant. They get to the Mississippi River and their wagon is one that has been pledged to go back and help bring out other Saints. They are deposited by a tree on the banks of the Mississippi River on the west bank.

"Martha says, 'To hear them, the children, crying at night with their feet cracked and bleeding was a grievous sight for a mother to bear.' So she greases their feet and puts clean socks on each of them. They are ice-bound for two weeks waiting to get across the river. Martha says that when they sent the wagon back, everything went out and landed by a log. So all of her belongings are in the snow next to a log. There is no wagon, and she's expecting. They are waiting for the ice to form so they can get across. It's not safe to walk. They've got to wait for a boat or a canoe to come over. Her husband, Daniel, rigs a rope bed for her under a tent made of quilts by a log fire. They wait for two weeks during a bad storm and the cornbread freezes so hard they have to use an ax to cut it." —**William G. Hartley**

Martha gave birth to a son whom they named Joseph, after the Prophet.[36]

Nancy Hammer, whose husband had been killed in the Hawn's Mill Massacre, moved her six children east in February. A blind horse pulled their small wagon. Her son John remembered the cold and frost and lack of wood for fires. The children "were almost barefooted and some had to wrap their feet in clothes in order to keep them from freezing and protect them from the sharp points of frozen ground, but often the blood from our feet marked the frozen earth." All but the two youngest children walked every step of the way.

The exodus continued during March. The accounts of travel even that late were grim. Eliza R. Snow left Far West on March 5. During that night the rain changed to snow. Their tent froze stiffly, so they could fold and pack it only after holding it by the fire and thawing it. The next day, the sun melted the snow and turned their road into mud.

Luman Shirtliff's group of two dozen people slept on frozen ground and needed big bonfires at night to keep warm.

On March 5, Bishop Partridge reported that ice had been running for three days so that no one could cross the Mississippi. Quincy, he said, was full of Mormons—even though

The Mormon refugees lined the western bank of the Mississippi River. Trapped against the river, they suffered greatly in the cold.

Refugees
by Kelly Donovon

Eliza R. Snow wrote of the suffering and cold of the Mormon exodus from Missouri.

Eliza R. Snow Photograph, attributed to Marsena Cannon, circa 1852. (Church History Library, Salt Lake City.) See http://www.josephsmithpapers.org/person/eliza-roxcy-snow

Latter-day Saints were scattering out from there almost constantly.[37]

Joseph Holbrook said a hundred men were along that west shoreline in mid-March.

Lyman Wight, a prisoner, learned in late March that his wife and six children were in a tent on the bank of the Mississippi without food and clothing.[38]

By March 20, Parley P. Pratt, just out of prison, went with his family to Far West, and there he found only "a few of the poor and widows and the Committee who tarried behind to assist them in removing."[39] His comments show that by the first day of spring, near March 21, the majority of the Missouri Saints had left Caldwell County.[40] Most, therefore, had traveled during wintertime.

Mormons had occasional contact with local Missourians. Some of the non-Mormons showed great compassion and charity, while others were rude and refused shelter, food, and even the use of dead tree limbs for fuel.

Final Removals: The Extermination Order Fulfilled

While small caravans were crossing Missouri during those winter weeks, the Committee on Removal continued to move the needy. On February 19 they sent Charles Bird to those outside Far West and William Huntington to those within Far West to find out which families needed help moving and to solicit means to aid the needy. On February 21, Bird identified seven families who needed assistance, and Huntington identified thirty-two.[41]

At a Church conference in Quincy on March 17, Elder Brigham Young spoke against scattering and urged the refugees to settle together in clusters. He read a letter from the Committee on Removal requesting that teams and money be sent back to remove fifty families who needed help.[42]

On April 11, David W. Rogers, working for the Committee on Removal, headed east from Far West; he took with him Parley P. Pratt's family, Brigham Young's mother-in-law, and two other women. At the Mississippi, Rogers found the water so high that they had to go down river several miles to find a place where a ferry could take them across.[43]

On April 14, the committee voted to send two women, a man, and another family with three teams that had recently arrived from Quincy. That same day, the committee moved thirty-six families to Tinney's Grove. The next day they made arrangements to move the last few remaining families from Far West.[44] On April 20, the last Mormon settlers left Far West.

> *Thus had a whole people, variously estimated at from ten to fifteen thousand souls, been driven from houses and lands and reduced to poverty, and had removed to another State during one short winter and part of a spring. The sacrifice of property was immense—including houses, lands, cattle, sheep, hogs, agricultural implements, furniture, household utensils, clothing, money and grain.*

By April 20, 1839, the last Latter-day Saint had left Far West. By 1907, when this George Edward Anderson photograph was taken, the town of Far West no longer existed.

Far West Temple Site by George Edward Anderson

One of the most flourishing counties in the State and part of several others were reduced to desolation, or inhabited only by marauding gangs.[45]

Meanwhile, seven Apostles secretly traveled to Far West and dedicated a temple site there on April 26–27.[46] Then, through the darkness, the men—not supposed to be in Missouri—went to Tinney's Grove and from there helped some last families needing help to reach Quincy. At that point, Brigham Young felt that the covenant to move the poor Saints had been fulfilled:

Mormon Redress Petition 1839. As commanded by revelation, Latter-day Saints filed with state and federal authorities a thousand petitions for redress, seeking compensation for their losses in the state of Missouri. The petitions received little notice. U.S. President Martin Van Buren said to the Prophet Joseph Smith, "Your cause is just, but I can do nothing for you."

We had entered into a covenant to see the poor Saints all moved out of Missouri to Illinois, that they might be delivered out of the hands of such vile persecutors, and we spared no pains to accomplish this object until the Lord gave us the desires of our heart. We had the last company of the poor with us that could be removed. Bros. P. P. Pratt and Morris Phelps were in prison, and we had to leave them for a season. We sent a wagon after Bro Yokum, who had been so dreadfully mutilated in the Haun's [sic] Mill massacre that he could not be moved. [47]

Not only was the covenant fulfilled, but so was Governor Boggs's extermination order—except, that is, for Latter-day Saints who'd found a safe haven in St. Louis.

Quincy Commemorative Marker: Latter-day Saints past and present have never forgotten the kindness of the people of Quincy in the winter of 1838–39.

Extermination's Legacies

This forced removal of seven to ten thousand Latter-day Saints was not without its short-term and long-term consequences, some of which were as follows:

(1) The Mormons suffered severe property losses, and their attempts to receive compensation failed. Their losses were not just in Caldwell County, but were compound losses incurred during eight years of living in and being forced from Missouri locations. Their petitions for redress, filed between 1839 and 1845, included

After 140 years, Missouri Governor Christopher Bond rescinded the Extermination Order in 1976.

EXECUTIVE OFFICE
STATE OF MISSOURI
JEFFERSON CITY

CHRISTOPHER S. BOND
GOVERNOR

FILED JUN 25 1976

SECRETARY OF STATE

EXECUTIVE ORDER

WHEREAS, on October 27, 1838, the Governor of the State of Missouri, Lilburn W. Boggs, issued an order calling for the extermination or expulsion of Mormons from the State of Missouri; and

WHEREAS, Governor Boggs' order clearly contravened the rights to life, liberty, property and religious freedom as guaranteed by the Constitution of the United States, as well as the Constitution of the State of Missouri; and

WHEREAS, in this Bicentennial year as we reflect on our nation's heritage, the exercise of religious freedom is without question one of the basic tenets of our free democratic republic;

NOW, THEREFORE, I, CHRISTOPHER S. BOND, Governor of the State of Missouri, by virtue of the authority vested in me by the Constitution and the laws of the State of Missouri, do hereby order as follows:

Expressing on behalf of all Missourians our deep regret for the injustice and undue suffering which was caused by this 1838 order, I hereby rescind Executive Order Number 44 dated October 27, 1838, issued by Governor Lilburn W. Boggs.

a thousand claims. Losses in Caldwell County alone, as listed in these petitions, included ten thousand acres of land and large losses of crops, livestock, tools, plows, wagons, bridles, harnesses, saws, axes, rifles, pistols, swords, fence rails, beds, blankets, quilts, tin plates, chairs, and tents. Additionally, affidavits said that the Missouri militia destroyed large amounts of timber, lumber, cattle, and hogs.[48]

(2) The Saints suffered physically. Some died of exposure while waiting to leave Missouri or soon afterward; among those were the fathers of Joseph Smith and Brigham Young. Many suffered ill health and weakness for months and even years as a result.

(3) The Saints' petitions and personal writings show that

Page 2

IN WITNESS WHEREOF: I have hereunto set my hand and caused to be affixed the great seal of the State of Missouri in the City of Jefferson on this 25th day of June, 1976.

GOVERNOR

ATTEST

SECRETARY OF STATE

they suffered mental and emotional wounds in Missouri and during the final expulsion. Their statements evince anger, horror, outrage, bitterness, and trauma.

(4) Thousands of displaced people had to go somewhere else. They did, and their presence and labor contributed to the development of farms, roads, livestock, settlements, services, commerce, and trade in Adams and Hancock counties, Illinois, and Lee County, Iowa,. The establishment of Nauvoo, Illinois, was a direct result of the Mormon expulsion from Missouri.

(5) Quincy gained an enhanced reputation for charitable treatment of oppressed groups. Joseph Smith expressed his people's regard in a thank-you letter published in the Quincy Whig on May 17, 1839, in which he thanked the people of Quincy for taking a stand against the lawless outrages of Missouri mobbers. He proposed that "favors of this kind ought to be engraved on the rock, to last forever." A historical marker in Quincy's city square has fulfilled that wish, as have printed

and audiovisual records of commemoration events held in Quincy.[49] Lasting regard for Quincy has endured in written and oral form among Mormon families who descend from the extermination victims who found brief refuge in Quincy.

(6) The 1838 Extermination Order formally existed for almost 140 years. On June 25, 1976, Missouri Governor Christopher S. Bond signed an executive order rescinding it and expressed "deep regret for the injustice and undue suffering" it caused. "Gov. Bogg's order clearly contravened the rights to life, liberty, property, and religious freedom as guaranteed by the Constitution of the State of Missouri," he declared.[50]

William G. Hartley

William G. Hartley is a retired Brigham Young University history professor. He's published widely about Mormon and western U.S. history, and is recipient of several best book and best article awards. He helped co-edit three volumes of the Joseph Smith Papers. He's a past president of the Mormon History Association.

ENDNOTES

1. Lilburn W. Boggs to John B. Clark, Oct. 27, 1838, *Document Containing the Correspondence, Orders, &c. in Relation to the Disturbances with the Mormons: And the Evidence Given Before the Hon. Austin A. King, Judge of the Fifth Judicial Circuit of the State of Missouri, at the court-House in Richmond, in a Criminal Court of Inquiry, Begun November 12, 1838, on the Trial of Joseph Smith, Jr., and Others, for High Treason and Other Crimes Against the State* (MO: Boone's Lick Democrat, 1841), 61. Extermination, a powerful word, means to eradicate but also implies killing.

2. This paper is an adaptation of my article, "'Almost Too Intolerable a Burthen': The Winter Exodus from Missouri, 1838–1839," *Journal of Mormon History* 18 (Fall 1992):6–40.

3. Alexander L. Baugh, "A Call to Arms: The 1838 Mormon Defense of Northern Missouri," PhD dissertation, Brigham Young University, 1996; Stephen LeSueur, *The 1838 Mormon War in Missouri* (Columbia, MO: University of Missouri Press, 1987); Leland H. Gentry, "A History of the Latter-day Saints in Northern Missouri from 1836–1839," PhD dissertation, Brigham Young University, 1965.

4. Baugh argues persuasively that the attackers had not heard about the Extermination Order; see Baugh, "A Call to Arms," 296–98.

5. Richard L. Anderson, "Clarification of Boggs' 'Order' and Joseph Smith's Constitutionalism," *Regional Studies in Latter-day Saint History: Missouri*, ed. Arnold K. Garr and Clark V. Johnson (Provo, UT: BYU Department of Church History, 1994), 27–83.

6. Anderson, "Clarification of Boggs' 'Order,'" 27.

7. Anderson, "Clarification of Boggs' 'Order,'" 49.

8. Journal History of The Church of Jesus Christ of Latter-day Saints, November 6, 1838, Church History Library.

9. *History of the Church*, 3:207; "Diaries of William Huntington," typescript copied by the BYU Library, 1953, in Miscellaneous Mormon Diaries, 16:6, L. Tom Perry Special Collections, Harold B. Lee Library, Brigham Young University, Provo, UT.

10. Anderson, "Clarification of Boggs' 'Order,'" 59; *History of the Church*, 3:430.

11. Stanley B. Kimball, "The Saints and St. Louis, 1831–1857: An Oasis of Tolerance," *BYU Studies* 13 (Summer 1973):489–519.

12. Journal History, Apr. 18, 1839.

13. John P. Greene, *Facts Relative to the Expulsion of the Mormons or Latter-day Saints from the State of Missouri, Under the "Exterminating Order"* (Cincinnati, OH: R. P. Brooks, 1839), 8.

14. "The Life of Joseph Holbrook, 1806–1871," typescript, 46, L. Tom Perry Special Collections.

15. Journal History, Nov. 6, 1832, 2.

16. Mary Ivers to parents, November 2 [?], 1844, Albert Brown Papers, copy on reel 10 in *Sources of Mormon History in Illinois, 1839–1848*, comp. Stanley B. Kimball (Southern Illinois University at Edwardsville). See Collection Guide, 16.

17. Lucy Mack Smith, *History of Joseph Smith by His Mother* (Salt Lake City: Stevens & Wallis, 1945), 292.

18. "Diaries of William Huntington," Typescript copied by the BYU Library, 1953, in Miscellaneous Mormon Diaries, Vol. 16, BYU Library

19. James Carroll, Petition, in Johnson, *Missouri Redress Petitions*, 155; see biographical sketch in *Far West Record*, ed. Donald Q. Cannon and Lyndon W. Cook (Salt Lake City: Deseret Book, 1983), 252.

20. Baugh, "A Call to Arms," 375.

21 Journal History, Dec. 28, 1838, and Jan. 5, 1839.

22 Journal History, Jan. 26, 1839.

23 *History of the Church*, 3:249–54, which includes names of those who pledged.

24 Dean C. Jessee and David J. Whittaker, eds., "The Last Months of Mormonism in Missouri: The Albert Perry Rockwood Journal," *BYU Studies* 28 (Winter 1988).

25 Journal History, Feb. 1, 1839.

26 Huntington, Diaries, 8.

27 Journal History, February 6 and 15, 1839.

28 B. H. Roberts, *A Comprehensive History of the Church of Jesus Christ of Latter-day Saints* (Provo, UT: BYU Press, 1965), 1:510–11.

29 Journal History, Nov. 6, 1838.

30 Greene, *Facts Relative to the Expulsion*, 40.

31 Hartley, "'Almost Too Intolerable a Burthen,'" 6–40.

32 Rockwood, Journal, 34.

33 L. Augustus Mitchell, "Map of the States of Missouri and Iowa and the Indian Territory," 1840, Cartography Collection, National Archives, Suitland, MD.

34 Smith, *History of Joseph Smith by His Mother*, 294–97.

35 Hartley, "'Almost Too Intolerable a Burthen,'" 25n63.

36 Hartley, "'Almost Too Intolerable a Burthen,'" 31n79.

37 Journal History, Mar. 5, 1839.

38 Lyman Wight, March 24, 1839. "Petition to L. W. Boggs [to be released from prison]," in Greene, *Facts Relative to the Expulsion*, 8.

39 Journal History, Mar. 20, 1839.

40 Hartley, "'Almost Too Intolerable a Burthen,'" 25.

41 Hartley, "'Almost Too Intolerable a Burthen,'" Feb. 15 and 21, 1839.

42 Hartley, "'Almost Too Intolerable a Burthen,'" Mar. 17, 1839.

43 Hartley, "'Almost Too Intolerable a Burthen,'" March 17, 1839. The Journal History introduction to this report by David W. Rogers is mistakenly dated February 1, 1839, but its internal contents show it was written in or after April 1839.

44 Hartley, "'Almost Too Intolerable a Burthen,'" Apr. 14–15, 1839.

45 Hartley, "'Almost Too Intolerable a Burthen,'" Apr. 20, 1839.

46 Hartley, "'Almost Too Intolerable a Burthen,'" Apr. 26, 1839.

47 Hartley, "'Almost Too Intolerable a Burthen.'"

48 Kenneth W. Godfrey, "New Light on Old Difficulties: The Historical Importance of the Missouri Affidavits," in *Regional Studies in Latter-day Saint Church History: Missouri*, 201–17.

49 Joseph Smith, Sidney Rigdon, and Hyrum Smith to Editors of the *Quincy Whig*, May 17, 1839, copied into Journal History, May 17, 1839.

50 Photocopy of order, filed June 25, 1976, copy in author's possession; see also transcript in *LDS Church News*, July 3, 1976, 4.

Joseph in Liberty Jail, by Gary E. Smith

Joseph Smith and fellow prisoners were incarcerated in Liberty Jail from December 1, 1838, to April 6, 1839, awaiting a formal hearing on the charge of treason against the state.

CHANGE OF VENUE

The Gallatin hearing and the escape of Joseph Smith and the Mormon prisoners from Missouri, April 1839

by Alexander L. Baugh

On April 6, 1839, Joseph Smith, his brother Hyrum, Caleb Baldwin, Alexander McRae, and Lyman Wight were taken from the jail in Liberty, Missouri, and placed in the custody of a strong guard assigned to transport them to Gallatin in Daviess County for what was expected to be a formal hearing on the charge of treason against the state. The Smiths and Wight had been in state custody for more than five months, Baldwin and McRae slightly less.

For more than four months the five men had languished in the loathsome Liberty dungeon. However, unbeknownst to them at the time, in fewer than three weeks they would be free men, reunited with their families and friends in Illinois. The Gallatin hearing, the release of Joseph Smith and his companions, and their flight across northern Missouri comprise one of the concluding chapters of the Mormon experience in Missouri.

The Arrest and Incarceration of the Mormon Prisoners

Following nearly three months of civil conflict between the Mormons and their Missouri neighbors, Joseph Smith, Sidney

Rigdon, George W. Robinson, Lyman Wight, and Parley P. Pratt were arrested at Far West, Caldwell County, Missouri, on October 31, 1838. The following day, Hyrum Smith and Amasa Lyman were also taken into custody. The arresting officers were actually part of the state militia called out by Governor Lilburn W. Boggs of Missouri to suppress and subdue the Mormons, arrest their leaders, and force their removal from the state.

Samuel Lucas, a major general in command of the state forces from Jackson and Lafayette counties, negotiated the Mormon surrender and made the arrests. Initially, Lucas and several other officers believed military law applied to the situation and ordered that the prisoners be court-martialed and executed. Fortunately, however, Alexander Doniphan, a brigadier general from Clay County and one familiar with both military and civil law, intervened. Doniphan knew that the Mormon leaders should be tried in civil court, and when he was ordered by Lucas to execute the prisoners, Doniphan refused. Frustrated, Lucas decided to transport the prisoners to Independence, where he would wait to receive further orders from his superior, Major General John B. Clark. Lucas and the prisoners arrived in Independence on November 4.

General Clark was a latecomer on the scene. On October 26, Governor Boggs relieved David R. Atchison of his command over the state militia of the northern district, replacing him with Clark, who was from Howard County in the central part of the state. By the time Clark arrived on the scene, the Mormons had already capitulated and Lucas had left, taking with him the Mormon prisoners. The commanding general

Major General Samuel D. Lucas ordered Brigadier General Alexander W. Doniphan to execute Joseph Smith and fellow prisoners. Doniphan refused.

I Will Not Obey Your Order by Robert T. Barrett

immediately sent word to Lucas that the prisoners were to be taken to Richmond, where they would undergo a preliminary hearing before the bench of Circuit Court Judge Austin A. King.[1]

Lucas left Independence with the Mormon leaders on November 8 and arrived at Richmond the following day. Meanwhile, General Clark, assisted by Captain Samuel Bogart of Clay County, rounded up additional Mormon men suspected of having been active participants in the events and campaigns of the Missouri conflict, placed them under arrest, and brought them to Richmond for the preliminary examination.

From November 12 through 29, sixty-four Mormons were arraigned before Judge King's court. In his final review of the case, King determined that sufficient evidence existed against Parley P. Pratt, Norman Shearer, Darwin Chase, Luman Gibbs, and Morris Phelps to charge them with murder in the death of Moses Rowland, which occurred at Crooked River during the skirmish between Mormon troops from Caldwell County and the Ray County militia commanded by Samuel Bogart. Since the charge of murder was a nonbailable offense, these five men were ordered to remain confined in the Richmond jail until the spring circuit court could convene. Later, King Follett was added to this group and charged with robbery. Probable cause was also found against Joseph Smith, Hyrum Smith, Sidney Rigdon, Lyman Wight, Alexander McRae, and Caleb Baldwin on the charge of treason—also a nonbailable offense. They were ordered to be taken to Liberty Jail in Clay County and imprisoned to await their court appearance.[2]

Leaving Richmond on November 30, the Smith brothers, Rigdon, Wight, McRae, Baldwin, and their guard arrived at Liberty the following day, which marked the beginning of their four-month confinement. In late January, the Mormon leaders were permitted a hearing before Clay County magistrate Judge Joel Turnham. Rigdon, who was ill, acted in his own defense and was released, while the remaining five prisoners were recommitted to jail pending notice to appear before a grand jury in Daviess County. Notification of the hearing came in early April.[3]

> In November 1838, Judge Austin A. King presided over the preliminary hearing held in Richmond, Missouri. At the outset, Judge King was heard to say, "If the Governor's exterminating order had been directed to me, I would have seen it fulfilled to the very letter ere this time."
>
> *Austin A. King*, Library of Congress, ca. 1862–63

Joseph Smith and fellow prisoners were charged with treason—a nonbailable offence—and transported to Liberty, Missouri, to await their court appearance.

Liberty Jail by G. Robinson Oborn

The Gallatin Hearing

On Saturday, April 6, the Clay County guard, under the direction of county sheriff Samuel Hadley, left Liberty bound for Gallatin with the Mormon Prophet and his fellow prisoners.[4] Peter H. Burnett and Amos Rees, two attorneys employed by the defendants, went along as counsel.[5] They made good time and distance the first day, traveling as far as Plattsburg in Clinton County, where they spent the night. On April 7, after traveling all day, they stopped and spent the night at the home of a woman named Taylor, who probably resided near Far West in Caldwell County.[6]

The following day, April 8, when the company was about a mile from Gallatin, they were met by William Morgan, the Daviess County sheriff, who took custody of the prisoners and allowed the Clay County guard to return.[7] The prisoners, accompanied by their new guard, arrived at Gallatin around noon. Hyrum Smith recorded that they were met by a large number of local town folk, "gazing & gaping [and] straining their eyes to see us."[8]

Following a midday meal, the prisoners were escorted about a mile south of town to the home of county treasurer Elisha B. Creekmore, where the trial was scheduled to be held.⁹ Here they were met by a more hostile gathering of men, who rushed upon them, cursing, swearing, and threatening to kill them. Unruffled, Joseph Smith was permitted to speak and quieted the crowd. "We are in your hands," he said; "if we are guilty, we refuse not to be punished by the law."

Hearing Joseph Smith's statement, William Peniston and William McKinney, bitter enemies of the Mormons, spoke to the people. "Yes, gentlemen, these men are in our hands; let us not use violence, but let the law have its course; the law will condemn them, and they will be punished by it; we do not want the disgrace of taking the law into our own hands."¹⁰ Joseph Smith's assurance that he would submit to the rule of the courts, along with Peniston's and McKinney's belief that justice would prevail, had a conciliating effect on the Daviess ruffians, and order was restored. The Prophet and his prison companions spent the rest of the day in counsel with their attorneys, Burnett and Rees.¹¹

In October 1838, during the height of the Mormon Missouri conflict, the Mormons had burned a handful of cabin structures and businesses in Gallatin, including the small log county courthouse. At the time of the hearing six months later, a new courthouse still had not been erected, so Elisha Creekmore's cabin home was chosen as the location for trial. The structure was not large—only about twenty-five feet square. At night the cabin also served as the sleeping quarters for the Mormon leaders, their attorneys, and their guard.¹² Although the accommodations were not the best, they were much better than what the prisoners had experienced while in Liberty Jail. Hyrum Smith noted that it was the first time he had slept in a bed in five months.¹³

Even though they now had beds, the prisoners did not get much restful sleep. One evening the guards stayed up all night drinking, playing cards, and cursing.¹⁴ On another night, they hooted and hollered until morning, and no one slept at

Peter Hardeman Burnett was one of Joseph Smith's defense attorneys. He was true to his charge. Years later Hardeman served as the first governor of the state of California.

Peter Hardeman Burnett, ca. 1860

On August 6, 1838, election day at the county seat of Gallatin, Missourians refused to give Mormons their constitutional right to vote. A brawl ensued that sparked the tinder of the Mormon War of 1838.

all.[15] Burnett, one of the attorneys, recalled, "As I slept in the room, I had an opportunity to see much of what passed. The prisoners did not sleep . . . for several nights."

Because of the constant clamor, Joseph Smith and Lyman Wight engaged in lengthy conversations, not only with each other but with a number of visitors. "By consent of the prisoners, many of the citizens of Davis [sic] came into the room, and conversed with them hour after hour during most of the night," Burnett recalled. Among the visitors were two ministers who came to engage the Mormon Prophet in a theological argument. However, Joseph Smith foresaw their objections and subsequently silenced them.[16]

Perhaps not surprisingly, the Prophet's mild-mannered temperament, cheerful disposition, and colorful personality helped him gain the friendship of the Daviess County rabble. One incident that helped him earn the respect of the guard occurred during a court recess. Knowing Joseph Smith's love of a good man-to-man wrestling match, someone suggested letting the Mormon Prophet grapple with John Brassfield, a member of the guard who had the distinction of being the strongest man in the county. Attorney Burnett recounted the incident:

Joseph Smith, Jr., was a very stout, athletic man, and was a skillful wrestler. This was known to the men of Davis [sic] County, and some of them proposed to Smith that he should wrestle with one of their own men. He at first courteously objected, alleging substantially that, though he was once in the habit of wrestling, he was now a minister of the gospel, and did not wish to do anything contrary to his duty as such, and that he hoped they would excuse him upon that ground. They kindly replied that they did not desire him to do anything contrary to his calling; that they would not bet anything; that it was nothing but a friendly trial of skill and manhood, for the satisfaction of others, and to pass away the time pleasantly; and that they hoped he would, under all the circumstances, comply with their request. He consented; they selected the best wrestler among them [John Brassfield], and Smith threw him several times in succession, to the great amusement of the spectators.[17]

Burnett was further intrigued at how the Mormon Prophet was able to almost completely disarm his antagonists. He wrote, "He [Joseph Smith] had great influence over others. . . . [At the end of the hearing] just before I left to return to Liberty, I saw him out among the crowd, conversing freely with everyone, and seeming to be perfectly at ease. In the short space of [four] days he had managed so to mollify his enemies that he could go unprotected among them without the slightest danger."[18]

On Tuesday, April 9, the day after arriving in Gallatin, the hearing convened before Judge Thomas C. Burch

While the court recessed, the guards urged Joseph Smith to engage in the friendly sport of wrestling. Joseph was reluctant, but after some insistence he agreed. Joseph bested a guard said to be the strongest man in the county.

The Wrestler by Glen S. Hopkinson

65

and a grand jury. Burch, a district attorney, had been the chief prosecuting attorney against the Mormons during the Richmond Court of Inquiry in November and had been appointed by Circuit Court Judge Austin A. King to adjudicate the case. Having prosecuted the earlier hearing, Burch was well aware of the charges being brought against the Mormon leaders.[19]

The Mormon defendants were particularly pleased when Josiah Morin arrived to witness the proceedings. Morin, who had previously served as a Daviess County judge, had befriended Joseph Smith and was sympathetic to the Mormon cause. He likely assisted and advised the defendants' attorneys in the case.[20] Other officers of the court were Robert Wilson, the county clerk, who acted as the court recorder, and Robert P. Peniston Jr., who was selected as jury foreman.

The twenty men who made up the grand jury were a sad group of frontier characters, though probably typical of the type of people who made up the local citizenry.[21] Hyrum Smith noted that the men who guarded them during the night were the same men who sat as jurors during the day.[22] However, their all-night partying and drinking caused a number to be incoherent when court was in session. At times, some

The diary of Hyrum Smith gives the names of Latter-day Saints who were killed or wounded in the massacre at Hawn's Mill.

Hawn's Mill Massacre by T. B. H. Stenhouse

jurors were so drunk that they were lifeless and had to be carried out of the room.²³

Because no formal records of the actual court testimony are known to exist, what transpired during the first day of proceedings is difficult to determine. However, a few short lines in Hyrum's diary reveal that the evidence presented on the first day may have focused on some of the destructive activities of the Mormons in Daviess County in September 1838.²⁴

April 10, the second day of the hearing, was spent in the examination of witnesses, only one of whom is mentioned by name in the historical sources: Sampson Avard, the noted Mormon Danite leader who had earlier been offered immunity by the state if he would testify in the Richmond hearing against the Church's leadership.²⁵ Other testimony rendered before Judge Burch is not known, although in Hyrum Smith's diary under this date is a full entry, giving the names of the Mormons who were killed or wounded at the Hawn's Mill Massacre in Caldwell County on October 30, 1838.²⁶ The defense was probably using the incident as evidence that the Missourians had committed crimes against the Mormons. Such testimony would have been even more damaging, especially in light of the fact that at least three of the men who were sitting as jurors—Nathaniel Blakely, John Brown, and Jacob S. Rogers—had been part of the vigilante force that had attacked the mill.²⁷

Peter H. Burnett observed Joseph Smith conversing freely with his enemies and moving among them without the slightest danger.

Foes Became His Friends by Gary Kapp

The examination of witnesses continued through April 11, the third and final day of the hearing. Again, the names of those who testified are not known, with the exception of Stephen Markham, who spoke in behalf of the defense. Markham's testimony must have incriminated James Blakely, because following an adjournment, Blakely physically assaulted Markham. Markham stood his ground even when ten men rallied to Blakely's defense. Fearing that he would be attacked on leaving Gallatin, Markham spent the night with the prisoners, arose early, and made a safe getaway.²⁸

At the conclusion of the court testimony, the defense requisitioned that Judge Burch issue a change of venue for the Mormon prisoners, arguing that he (Burch) should not be allowed to rule in this case, since he had been the prosecuting attorney against the Mormon prisoners at the Richmond hearing in November.[29] The defense counsel also requested that the change of venue be made to Marion County, located on the eastern border of the state and opposite Adams County, Illinois (where the majority of the Saints had relocated).[30] The hearing ended when Burch upheld the request for a change of venue but ordered that the hearing for the defendants be moved not to Marion County, but to Boone County, in the center of the state.[31]

The Release

The Daviess County guard assigned by Judge Burch to take the Mormon prisoners to Columbia, Boone County, Missouri, included Sheriff William Morgan, William Bowman (Bowman had been the first sheriff of Daviess County), John Brassfield (the Prophet's wrestling opponent), John Pope, and Wilson McKinney.[32] Unlike the previous moves between jails, which were accompanied by a heavy guard, this transfer involved an escort of only five men.

Around two o'clock on the afternoon of Wednesday, April 12, the party left Gallatin. The Daviess guards were on horses, while the five prisoners rode in a two-horse wagon. The company did not immediately begin the hundred-mile journey to Boone County, but instead traveled five miles north to Adam-ondi-Ahman, where they spent the night at William Bowman's residence. Significantly, Bowman's cabin had previously belonged to Lyman Wight. Both Bowman and Morgan were early settlers in Grand River Township and were close neighbors to the Saints at Diahman. Following the Mormon surrender, it appears Bowman laid claim to some of Wight's property.[33] The purpose of the layover was probably so Morgan and Bowman could procure some belongings and get outfitted before starting on the journey. The officers probably intended to leave Diahman the next morning (April 13), but rain caused them to delay their departure until the following day.³⁴

On Sunday, April 14, the company set out once again, but traveled only as far as Millport, a distance of approximately seven miles, where they stayed at the home of Josiah Morin, the ex-judge of Daviess who had befriended Joseph Smith. On this date, Hyrum Smith noted in his journal, "things tend to be favorable to us[,] the gard [sic] very lenient and kind the weather fair & pleasant."³⁵

Leaving Morin's home on the morning of April 15, the company traveled east into Livingston County via the main road connecting Gallatin and Chillicothe on the north side of the Grand River. They stopped that night at the home of a family named Cox, who Hyrum noted were "Mormon eaters."³⁶

The following day, the company made good time, traveling nineteen miles.³⁷ During their travels they were loosely guarded, and occasionally the group became separated. Lyman Wight stated, "after traveling three days, the Sheriff and I were together by ourselves five miles from . . . the rest of the company."³⁸ Such complacency on the part of the Daviess guard indicates that Bowman and Morgan had every intention of letting the prisoners go once they were a sufficient distance from the predominantly anti-Mormon Daviess and Livingston counties.

On Tuesday, April 16, the guard and prisoners stopped for the night at a location near Yellow Creek in Chariton County.³⁹ It was at this point that the prisoners were allowed to escape.⁴⁰ Here, Sheriff Morgan informed Lyman Wight "that he wished to God he was at

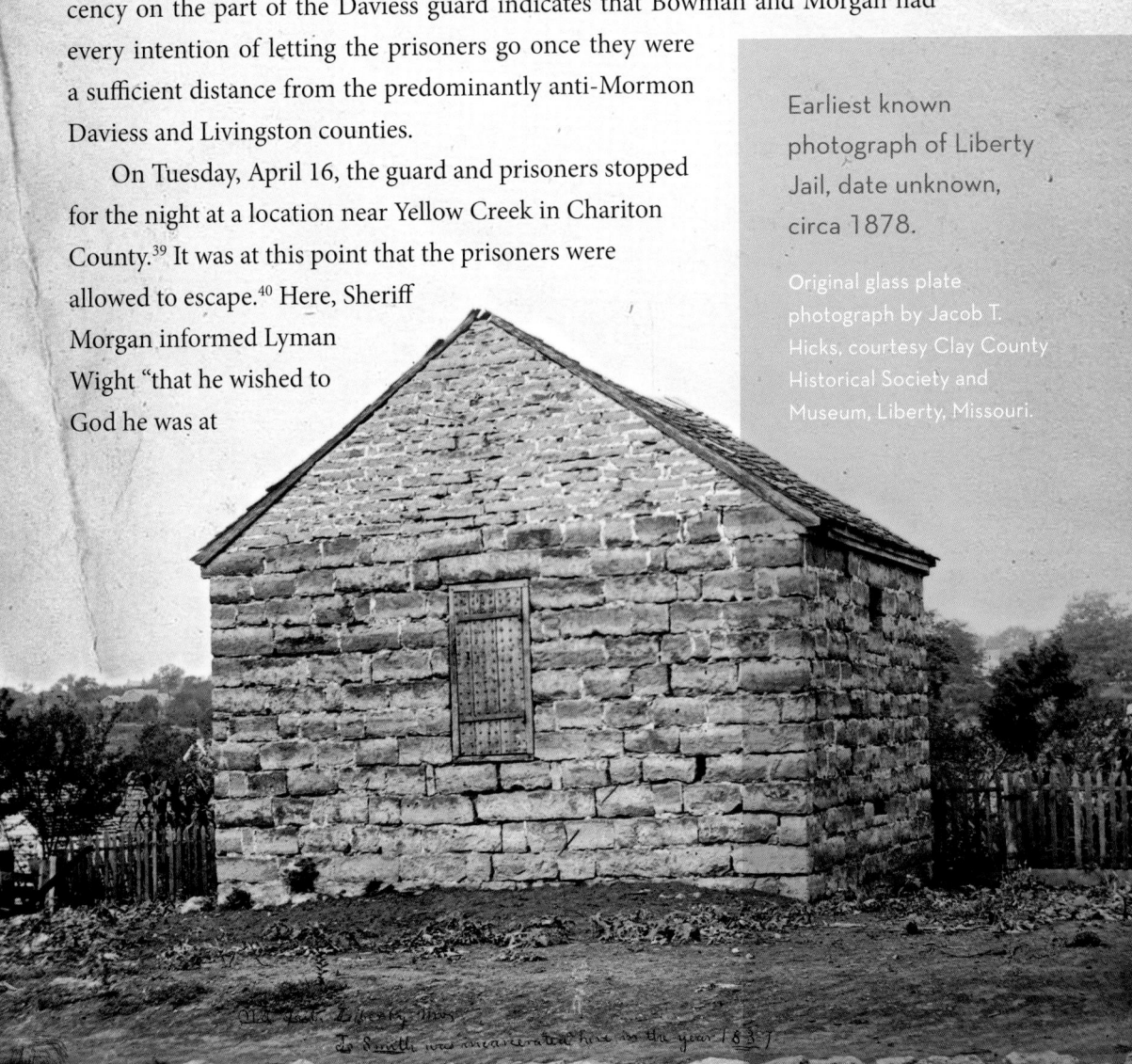

Earliest known photograph of Liberty Jail, date unknown, circa 1878.

Original glass plate photograph by Jacob T. Hicks, courtesy Clay County Historical Society and Museum, Liberty, Missouri.

home, and your friends also," then added, "By G__, I shall not go much further."⁴¹ Hyrum Smith testified that Morgan told them that Judge Burch instructed him "never to carry us to Boone County."

The Mormon prisoners had earlier purchased a jug of whiskey, which they gave that night to the five Daviess men. "Three . . . of the guard drank pretty freely of the whiskey," Hyrum Smith reported. "They also went to bed, and were soon asleep." Shortly afterward, Sheriff Morgan told them, "I shall take a good drink of grog and go to bed . . . and you may do as you have a mind to." He and another guard provided them with two horses and then helped them load the animals with their belongings.⁴² Joseph Smith wrote, "the guard got intoxicated, [and] we thought it a favorable opportunity to make our escape. . . . We took the advantage of the situation . . . and took our departure."⁴³ In recounting the event four years later, Hyrum stated (perhaps in jest), "We took our change of venue to the state of Illinois."⁴⁴

The five men wasted no time in getting away. "[We] traveled all knight [sic]," Hyrum wrote, "watered our horses & continued our journey till about 12 o clock [the next day]."⁴⁵ With only two horses among the five of them, they did not

At the conclusion of the grand jury hearing, Joseph and fellow prisoners traveled under guard five miles north to Adam-ondi-Ahman, where they spent the night in the cabin that had been the home of Lyman Wight.

Lyman Wight's Cabin at Adam-ondi-Ahman by Al Rounds

travel quickly. Most of the time only two could ride, while the other three had to keep up as best they could by walking. Joseph was one of the first to take his turn traveling on foot. "When we escaped," he later remarked, "I jumped into the mud, [then] put on my boots without working [them on] and when I got to water after going over 15 miles [of] prairie my boots were full of blood."[46]

With the prisoners free to make their way to Quincy, the next morning the Daviess officers continued their journey a few miles to Keytesville, where they took breakfast with Sterling Price, Chariton County's representative in the Missouri legislature, before returning to Gallatin.[47] Between Keytesville and Gallatin, the Daviess guard met up with David W. Rogers, a Mormon. In talking with the five Daviess officers, Rogers learned some of the particulars about the release of Joseph Smith and the four others.

Lyman Wight noted that the guard was loose and complacent and that the sheriff intended to let the Mormon prisoners go free.

Before the officers moved on, John Brassfield—the guard who had wrestled Joseph Smith during the Gallatin hearing—showed his light-hearted side. Brassfield was not only a brawler, but also a fiddler, and he played Rogers a tune he had composed about the Mormon leader. He told Rogers, "When you see . . . Smith tell him for me if I ever find him I will play him the tune called Jo Smith. [He] then began to pass the horse hair over the cat gut saying thats it."[48]

Exactly when Morgan, Bowman, and the three other guards arrived at Gallatin is not certain. However, their early return was a clear indication to the local townspeople that the Mormon leaders had gotten away. Morgan reported to the citizens that the prisoners had escaped during the night, taking the horses, and that a search for them had proved unsuccessful. But their version of events did not sit well with some of the angry local citizens, who accused Morgan and Bowman of aiding and abetting in the Mormon prisoners' so-called escape. The rabble specifically singled out Bowman, subjecting him to harsh punishment by tying him to a steel rail and dragging him through the streets. Tragically, the injuries he incurred from this ordeal led to his death a short time later.[49]

Why Sheriff Morgan did not receive the same treatment is not clear; perhaps it was because Bowman was specifically entrusted with safeguarding the prisoners, while Morgan went along to oversee the transfer. Thus Bowman, and not Morgan, was ultimately responsible for their getting away.[50]

In July, two and a half months after the incident, Morgan penned a document declaring that in taking charge of the Mormon prisoners he had acted responsibly and that he should not be accountable for the prisoners getting away. He wrote:

In response to the outrage of the local citizenry, Sheriff William Morgan penned an affidavit absolving himself of any blame for the release of the Mormon prisoners.

Preamble

Whereas many reports are in circulation relative to the escape of the mormon prisoners, from the Sheriff of this County, on his way from here, to Columbia, where he was conveying them to gaol, which have created and confirmed the suspicion of this meeting that their escape was not accidental nor unavoidable; but on the contrary, from facts within our own knowledge and all the circumstances taken together we are forced to adopt the opinion that they were willfully set at liberty. Yet from the fact that the evidence upon which this meeting bases its opinion of the guilt of the sheriff might not, in a court of law, be admitted, or not sufficient to convict them (the Sheriff & his guard) and thus subject them to that punishment they deserve, and that the law would inflict. Therefore an expression of opinion on this subject should be made publickly to the world, condemning and reprobating the conduct of the actors in this disgracefull affair and hold them up to the contempt of all good and honourable citizens. The most favourable construction that can posebly be put on this unfortunate affare is, that the Sheriff was guilty of a palpable and willfull neglect of his official duty. Infact the whole tenor of his official conduct

This is to certify that I executed the written order by taking the bodys [sic] of Caleb Baldwin Lyman Wight Joseph Smith Jr into my custody and that I sumoned [sic] a guard of four men to wit William Bowman Wilson McKinney John Brassfield and John Pope to assist me in taking the said Smith Wight and others from E B. Creekmores in the County of Daviess to the town of Columbia in the County of Boone State of Missouri as commanded by said order and that on the way from said E B Creekmores in the County of Daviess to the town of Columbia aforesaid on the 16th day of April 1839 the Smith Wight and others made their escape without the common concent [sic] or negligence of myself or said gard [sic].

> *July 6th 1839*
> *William Morgan Sheriff*
> *Of Daviess County*[51]

When Parley P. Pratt learned that Joseph Smith and the other Mormon prisoners had escaped, he worried that the escape might hinder his quest for justice.

Morgan's statement contradicts the historical evidence. He never had any intention of delivering Joseph Smith and his companions to Columbia, Missouri. Furthermore, he not only allowed them to escape but did in fact aid them in their efforts. With his reputation tarnished as a result of the incident, Morgan left the county a short time later.[52]

News of the so-called escape spread rapidly throughout the northern counties and was the subject of much written exchange. Richmond was one of the first communities to receive word. In fact, when Parley P. Pratt (who was awaiting trial in Richmond along with Darwin Chase, Norman Shearer, Morris Phelps, Luman Gibbs, and King Follett) first learned of the escape, he was concerned that the incident might have a bearing on the decision associated with their upcoming hearing. Writing to his wife, Mary Ann, on April 21, just five days after the so-called escape, Pratt wrote:

> *It is reported here, and generally believed by the people, that the Liberty prisoners have all escaped from the guards, while on their way to Columbia. If this is trew [sic], I know not what effect it may have upon the people here in regard to their feelings towards us; nor what effect it may have on our trials. There seems to be but little excitement on the subject as yet. Some say, "Dam [sic] them, let them go." Others say that, if they had Smith, they would not care for all the rest.*[53]

William Barbee, a resident of Carroll County, writing to his wife's relative Thomas Bradford in Virginia, gave some significant details about the escape:

> *I presume you are anxious to hear how the Mormons are getting along from information from the upper Counties they have nearly all gone and are getting off as fast as possible[.] there were 5 prisoners who have been confined in Clay County Jail[,] got a removal of their trial to Boone County and one day last week about 12 miles north of this [place] the sheriff who had charge of them suffered them all to escape (no doubt intentionally) among the prisoners were Joe Smith the prop[h]et and his brother . . . [who] were charged with murder, arson & treason[.]*[54]

Writing from Elkhorn, Missouri, on April 22, Samuel Bogart—the notorious captain who commanded the Ray County contingent against the Caldwell County Mormon militia at Crooked River, and who later apprehended a number of Latter-day Saints to appear before Judge King in Richmond—wrote the Quincy postmaster, informing him among other things of the purported getaway. "It is rumured [sic] here that Joseph Smith & the four other prisoners . . . made thare [sic] escape from the guard who [were] guarding them to Columbia, Boon[e] County. I think the report is tru[e]."[55]

Isaac J. Harvey, writing from Knavesville to his wife in

W. W. Phelps believed the rumor that Joseph Smith and fellow prisoners bribed the guards to gain their freedom. The rumor was unsubstantiated.

Indiana, reported, "Jo. Smith and others have made their escape from the Sheriff & guard by stealing two of thair [sic] best horses. It is said that Smith had 20 thousand dollars in jaoil [sic] with him. The general opinion is the horses was well sold."[56] A similar letter was written by W. W. Phelps to his wife, Sally, who was living in Dayton, Ohio. Phelps, a prominent Latter-day Saint who was the Church's first printer and who later served in the Missouri presidency, became disaffected from Mormonism shortly after the Mormon capitulation. Because of his dissociation from the Church, Phelps was not required to leave Missouri and maintained his residence in Far West. When word of the purported escape reached him, he wrote Sally to inform her of the news. In a second letter to Sally dated May 1, 1839, he repeated some additional rumors that were circulating. "Since I wrote to you about the escape of Joseph and Co. it has been reported that he bribed the guard with six thousand dollars," he wrote. Then he added, "I presume he did."[57] He obviously believed the rumor.

W. W. Phelps

The reports by Harvey and Phelps raise an interesting question: Did the Mormon prisoners bribe the guards in exchange for their freedom? In a statement by Alexander Doniphan that appeared in the *Chicago Times,* Doniphan said that Alanson Ripley, a Church agent who had been sent back to Missouri to sell some of the Mormon landholdings, had given Joseph Smith $900 prior to their leaving Gallatin. Using the money, Joseph struck a bargain to pay Sheriff Morgan $1,100 for their release, giving $700 in payment and a promissory note for the remaining $400.[58] However, this was not the case. Joseph also certainly did not have the $20,000 Harvey claimed, nor the $6,000 Phelps stated, nor even the $900 mentioned by Doniphan. David W. Rogers, a Latter-day Saint, indicated that Alanson Ripley indeed delivered some money to the prisoners while they were at Gallatin, but it totaled only $150.[59]

An examination of the sources reveals that when the officers informed the Mormon prisoners that they intended to release them, Joseph and his companions were also induced to give them some sort of payment in exchange for their freedom. During their two-day layover at Bowman's cabin in Diahman, the prisoners had made arrangements to secure the two horses used in their transport.

Hyrum Smith stated that they gave a note for one animal and some clothing for another.[60] Joseph H. McGee, a Gallatin resident, wrote that it was John Brassfield who made the arrangements to provide the horses for the Mormons.[61] As noted, the prisoners were not able to make full payment for the two animals. Furthermore, it is unlikely that they had the amount requested by the guard in exchange for their release.

On April 16, just before they were released, Joseph Smith struck a written promissory note to Brassfield pledging full payment for the animals. The note reads: "Promise to pay John Brassfield one hundred and fifty Dollars for value received. Given under my hand and seal This 16th Day of April 1839."[62] A second note of some unknown amount was also agreed upon in exchange for the prisoners' freedom. Within a day or two, the guard received partial payment from Heber C. Kimball. Elder Kimball, who was still in the process of trying to remove from the state, met up with the returning Daviess posse and later wrote: "At Tenny's a man [probably Brassfield] came to me and presented an order drawn on me by Joseph Smith for five hundred dollars, saying it was for the horses furnished him. I immediately raised four hundred dollars and paid him."[63] Actually, the note Kimball signed was probably for their freedom, not the horses.

In February 1843, nearly four years after Joseph Smith and his cellmates fled Missouri, John Brassfield (and perhaps others of the guard) traveled to Nauvoo and received the remainder of his remuneration. On February 28, 1843, the Prophet's history states that he spent the day with his mother and family and "Mr. John Brassfield, with whom I became acquainted in Missouri."[64] Joseph Smith III remembered the reason for Brassfield's visit was connected to the horses and the escape plan:

> When Father came to Quincy from his imprisonment in Missouri he brought with him a fine saddle horse–a dark chestnut sorrel stallion, named Medley, which he had obtained from the men who guarded them at the time of their escape. From circumstances which I remember in

In February 1843, John Brassfield, one of the guards who allowed Joseph Smith and the other Mormon prisoners to escape, came to Nauvoo to collect on the Prophet's promissory notes.

76

connection therewith I have reason to believe it had been purchased at a good figure. Whether or not Uncle Hyrum had also received a horse I cannot now say, but I remember that after the passage of some time, two men came to the house to see Father, one of whom was named John Brassfield. I understood at the time that these men had come for the purpose of collecting the amount of the bribe for which they had allowed the prisoners to escape. I cannot fix this date in memory other than to say it was after the erection of what was called the Red Brick Store, located in the west end of the block on which our house stood.

I remember hearing at the time that the amount of money to be paid these men was eight hundred dollars, and that the horse Father had owned was to be replaced by another. I remember the cream-colored or "clay-bank" horse which Father purchased from Amos Davis for the purpose of turning over to these men from Missouri. They were closeted [boarded] with Father and one or two others for the afternoon and part of the evening, and departed the next day.[65]

Joseph III's use of the word *bribe* should be taken in context with the entire ordeal. As has been discussed, the actions of Morgan, Bowman, and the other guards indicate that they had no intention of delivering the Mormon prisoners to Boone County, but had in fact been instructed by Judge Burch to release them at some appropriate time and place. Thus, prior to their departure, the guards had predetermined that they would let the prisoners go. Given such intentions on the part of the Daviess officers, it

Joseph Smith's Nauvoo Homestead.

Approximate route of Joseph Smith and the other Mormon prisoners to Quincy.

cannot be construed that the Mormon prisoners bribed the guard, but rather agreed to their terms.

Flight to Quincy

The route that Joseph Smith and his companions traveled as they made their way from Yellow Creek in Chariton County, Missouri, to Quincy, Illinois, cannot be precisely determined. However, at the time of their escape they were south of the main northern road that ran in nearly a direct line east from Chillicothe to Palmyra (present-day Missouri State Highway 36 closely follows this route). They were also north of a primary southern east-west route that passed through Tinney's Grove, Keytesville, Huntsville, and Paris before it turned in a northeastern direction toward Monroe City (present-day State Road 24 from Keytesville follows this route). These were well-traveled roads that were the primary routes taken by sev-

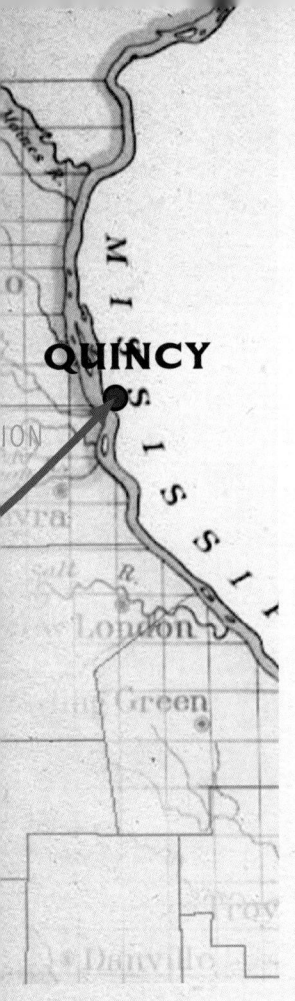

eral thousand Mormons during their exodus from the state in early 1839.⁶⁶ The refugees purposely avoided these thoroughfares, anticipating that when the word spread that they were on the loose, patrols would be sent along these lines to try to recapture them. Hyrum Smith recorded in his diary that the day after their release they abandoned the idea of traveling on the main roads and "took to the prairie" until reaching the Mississippi crossing.⁶⁷ Examining the line between Yellow Creek and Quincy, the Prophet and his companions probably traveled due east through Chariton, Randolph, and Monroe counties, then traversed in a northeasterly direction through Marion County before arriving at the Mississippi crossing, opposite Quincy.⁶⁸

The day following their release (April 17), Caleb Baldwin became separated from the group. While traveling, they noticed a man approaching; thinking he may be someone on the lookout for them, they split up and sought cover. Baldwin hid in some hazel brush until all was clear, but when it was time to move on, the others could not find him. Rather than wait, the four continued on another five miles before Hyrum Smith sent Alexander McRae on a horse to try to find Baldwin. McRae returned without success. The foursome believed it best to press forward with the hope that their lost companion would catch up or find his way by himself. The refugees traveled well into the night until, needing both rest and food, they rested on the prairie grass under the open sky.

The next day (Thursday, April 18), following a second hard day of overland travel, the four men arrived at the home of George Harris, a Latter-day Saint living on the Chariton River. Here they enjoyed a restful night among friends. The next morning, "to our astonishment," Hyrum Smith wrote, "bro baldwin came in he had traveled all knight [sic] in the wilderness & providentialy [sic] came to us."⁶⁹

Little is known about what happened between the time the Mormon refugees left the Harris home on the Chariton River and arrived at Quincy four days later. The Prophet's history states that they continued on their journey, traveling "both by night and by day; suffering much fatigue and hunger."⁷⁰

One humorous incident occurred during this time. As noted, they tried to take precautions to avoid detection. Orange L. Wight, Lyman Wight's son, remembered that they not only tried to travel inconspicuously, but also incognito, posing as land seekers and using fake names. They knew if they used their real names they could be identified, tracked down, and even arrested. Orange mentioned only the name Alexander McRae went by—Brown—but not the pseudonyms used by Joseph, Hyrum, Caleb, or his father.

One evening during the last leg of their journey across the state (between April 19 and 21), the Mormon men encountered a rural farmer who provided them lodging for the night. The next morning, the farmer engaged McRae in a conversation and asked what his name was. McRae's mind went blank; he couldn't remember what name he had decided to use. Not wanting to arouse suspicion, McRae immediately diverted the farmer's question by pretending he was ill with a terrible stomach cramp. The distraction worked.

Concerned, the farmer immediately left McRae and sought out Joseph and the others, informing them that their friend was very sick and in need of attention. Finding McRae, one of the party reminded McRae of his fake name by asking, "Mr. Brown, what is the matter with you, what have you been eating[?]" With that bit of information, McRae immediately began to feel better. The benevolent man recommended McRae drink a glass of whiskey to settle his stomach, then gave each of the others a round of the whiskey in case the sickness was contagious.[71]

A final incident occurred on April 21, the day before their arrival in Quincy. Alexander McRae and Joseph Smith apparently had a misunderstanding of some sort. Sparing detail, Lyman Wight's journal entry reads simply, "McRae left us, being displeased with Joseph."[72]

The following day, April 22, was joyous and eventful for each of the men. The Prophet and Caleb Baldwin took the horses and raced on ahead of Hyrum and Lyman Wight. They were the first to reach the river crossing opposite Quincy, arriving early in the morning.[73] Dimick B. Huntington was at the landing and was the first to see Joseph. He wrote:

> *I Dimick Huntington saw Joseph land from the Quincy ferry boat about 8 oc. in morning. He was drest in an*

old pair of boots full of holes, pants torn, tucked inside of boots, blue cloak with collar turned up, wide brim black hat, rim sloped down, not been shaved for some time, looked pale & haggard. I Dimick rode down at the request of Emma to enquire the news if any, from the west. When I got within about 16 ft. of him he raised his head. I exclaimed My God is it you Bro. Joes. He raised his hand & stopped me saying Hush, Hush. He then asked where is my family. I told him they were 4 miles east at Judge Clevelands in a room I had provided for them. I asked him if he wished to see his father & mother as they were in Quincy. He said no it would be too great a shock, they are old & cannot bear it. Take me to my family as quick as you can. In passing through the back streets of Quincy a number of men knew him. On arriving at the house where his family was Emma knew him as he was dismounting from his horse. She met him half way to the gate. Joseph not knowing the universal friendly feelings that existed in Quincy, was fearful he might be arrested again.[74]

Joseph's history simply states, "I arrived in Quincy, Illinois, amidst the congratulations of my friends, and the embraces of my family."[75] Hyrum and Lyman Wight arrived around six p.m. that same day.

A Quincy newspaper reporter publicized the arrival of Joseph Smith and his prison companions, concluding with a favorable description of the Church President and Prophet:

When Joseph Smith stepped ashore in Quincy, Dimick Huntington was the first man to greet him. He described the Prophet looking "pale & haggard."

> The celebrated Mormon leader, Joseph Smith, who has so long been in confinement in the upper part of Missouri, arrived in town on Monday last. He and four of his companions, consisting of Lyman Wight, Caleb Baldwin, Hiram Smith and Alexander McRae, escaped from the guard which was taking them from Daviess to Boone county for trial. The guard got drunk and fell asleep, on one night of their travel, and the prisoners knowing that they could not expect justice in any of the courts of upper Missouri, very properly turned their backs upon their persecutors and left them alone in their iniquity. We had supposed from the stories and statements we had read of "Jo Smith" (as he is termed in the papers)

to find him a very illiterate, uncouth sort of a man; but from a long conversation, we acknowledge an agreeable disappointment. In conversation, he appears intelligent and candid, and divested of all malicious thought and feeling towards his relentless persecutors.[76]

Joseph Smith's arrival at Quincy ended an arduous ten-day, 170-mile journey from Gallatin, Missouri, to the Mississippi, but it also marked the end of a denigrating and disparaging incarceration. The Missouri experience was a bitter pill not only for the Mormon leader, but for the entire Church. However, the welcome that both he and his followers received from the citizens of Quincy offered new hope that better days were ahead. As Joseph wrote:

Joseph and Emma: The Reunion
by A.D. Shaw

> *I was ... a Prisoner about six months, but notwithstanding their determination to destroy me, with the rest of my brethren who were with me; ... yet through the mercy of God, in answer to the prayers of the Saints, I have been preserved, and delivered out of their hands, and can again enjoy the society of my friends and brethren, whom I love; and to whom I feel united in bonds that are stronger than death; and in a State where I believe the laws are respected, and whose citizens are humane and charitable.*[77]

Were the Mormon Prisoners Fugitives from Justice?

One final question should be asked: Were Joseph and Hyrum Smith, Lyman Wight, Caleb Baldwin, and Alexander McRae fugitives from justice? Certainly the citizens in Missouri's northern counties believed so, since the Mormon prisoners escaped while en route to their trial in Boone County. However, a closer examination reveals that the civil officials never had any intention to fully prosecute them.

Within a short time after the Mormon surrender on November 1, 1838, Governor Boggs and Circuit Court Judge Austin King apparently became satisfied that once the Mormons left the state, the prisoners would be let go. At least two factors likely contributed to such a decision. First, how could the state actively incarcerate and prosecute only the Mormons without taking similar action against the Missourians, especially since it was well known that the Missourians had been involved in illegal activities and had committed terrible crimes against the Mormons? Second, while some approved of the governor's actions, the entire Mormon affair was essentially an embarrassment to the Boggs administration and the entire state; therefore, the sooner the whole affair was put completely to rest and the Mormon prisoners were released and gone, the better.

> After months of separation, Joseph Smith and his wife Emma had a joyful reunion at the home of Judge John Cleveland.

Sufficient evidence exists to show that Boggs and King never intended to fully prosecute Joseph Smith and his associates. This decision may have been reached within a matter of only a few days following the Mormon capitulation. Evidence for this comes from John B. Clark, the militia general appointed by Governor Boggs to oversee the operation during the last few days of the Mormon War. Clark stated that Judge King told him the Mormon leaders "were to be put in prison, but were not to be guarded too closely, and if they got away and left the state, they would be allowed to go."[78]

Following the Richmond hearing in late November, as the prisoners were being taken to Liberty, one of the men in charge of the prisoners informed them that "the Judge [Austin King] had made out a *mittimus* and sentenced us to jail for treason. He also said the Judge declared his intention to keep us in jail until all the 'Mormons' were driven from the state. He also said that the Judge had further declared that if he let us out before the 'Mormons' had left the state . . . there would be another damned fuss kicked up."[79] This explains why Judge King charged Joseph Smith and the others with treason. Treason was a nonbailable offense, which meant that they had to remain in custody until the regular court hearing was held, which was not scheduled until spring. In the meantime, it was anticipated that the Latter-day Saint population would make their way out of Missouri. Then, once the Mormons complied and left the state, the leaders would be released.[80] Part of how this happened is revealed by Hyrum Smith, who wrote:

> The jailer [at Liberty Jail], Samuel Tillery, Esq., told us . . . that the whole plan was concocted by the governor down to the lowest judge in that upper country. . . . He told us that the governor was now ashamed of the whole transaction and would be glad to set us at liberty if he dared do it. "But," said he, "you need not be concerned, for

The injustice of Missouri played out for many years in their lives. It was a time of deep hardship, and I'm amazed at their resilience. I think what's even more significant to me is how many remained true and faithful. Yeah, we lost a few. But they moved on, picked up the pieces, and started over again. But they didn't forget. And Missouri—they were glad to be gone from Missouri. We should never forget what they went through. But again, the time has passed. We don't need to dwell on the terribleness, the atrocities, the things that transpired, so much as we need to remember that they lived through it, did the best they could, tried to work things out, and hoped that God would deliver them and give them a new start and make things good again." —*Alexander L. Baugh*

the governor has laid a plan for your release. He also said that Squire Birch [sic] . . . was appointed to be circuit judge on the circuit passing through Daviess county, and that he (Birch) was instructed to fix the papers, so that we would be sure to be clear from any incumbrance [sic] in a very short time.[81]

Thus the plan went as follows: First, Governor Boggs instructed Judge King to structure things so the Mormon prisoners would be released after the Mormon populace had complied with the Extermination Order and left the state. To ensure this, King charged the Mormon defendants with treason during the Richmond hearing and ordered them to Liberty Jail. In the spring of 1839, King ordered the prisoners' grand jury trial be held in Gallatin and appointed Thomas Burch, the state's prosecuting attorney in the Richmond hearing (which King himself conducted), to preside at the Gallatin court. King also instructed Burch to "fix the papers" so that the prisoners could be conveniently let go. Burch complied by granting a change of venue to Columbia so that the prisoners could be released en route to Boone County. Finally, as has been demonstrated, before leaving Gallatin for Columbia, the Daviess guards were instructed by Burch to let the prisoners go at some convenient location. In short, Governor Boggs and Judges King and Burch acted together and arranged for the release of the Mormon Prophet, his brother Hyrum, Caleb Baldwin, Alexander McRae, and Lyman Wight. This plan eventually became known to the prisoners themselves, who later testified, "by order of the Governor of the State of Missouri, [they] were set at large, with directions to leave the State without delay."[82]

Alexander L. Baugh

Alexander L. Baugh is a professor in the Department of Church History and Doctrine at BYU. He received his BS from Utah State University, and his MA and PhD degrees from Brigham Young University. He specializes in researching and writing about the Missouri period of early LDS Church history (1831–1839). He is the author, editor, or co-editor of seven books, and he has published over eighty historical journal articles, essays, book chapters, and book reviews. He is a member of the Mormon History Association and the John Whitmer Historical Association, having served as president of that organization in 2006–2007. He is also the past editor of *Mormon Historical Studies*. He currently serves as the co-director of research for the Religious Studies Center at BYU, and he is a volume editor for the Joseph Smith Papers.

ENDNOTES

1. For a detailed documented discussion on the arrest of the Mormon prisoners, see Alexander L. Baugh, "The Mormon Surrender at Far West" and "Surrender and Military Occupation" in *A Call to Arms: The 1838 Mormon Defense of Northern Missouri* (Provo, UT: Joseph Fielding Smith Institute for Latter-day Saint History and BYU Studies, 2000), 135–70.

2. For an examination of the Richmond preliminary hearing, see Stephen C. LeSueur, "'High Treason and Murder': The Examination of Mormon Prisoners at Richmond, Missouri, in November 1838," *BYU Studies* 26, no. 2 (Spring 1986):3–30; Alexander L. Baugh, "The Final Episode of Mormonism in Missouri in the 1830s: The Incarceration of the Mormon Prisoners in Richmond and Columbia Jails, 1838–1839," *John Whitmer Historical Association Journal* 28 (2008):1–34; Alexander L. Baugh, "'Tis Not for Crimes That I Have Done': Parley P. Pratt's Missouri Imprisonment, 1838–1839," in *Parley P. Pratt and the Making of Mormonism*, ed. Gregory Armstrong, Matthew J. Grow, and Dennis J. Siler (Norman, OK: Arthur H. Clark Company, 2011), 137–67; and Alexander L. Baugh, "'Silence, Ye Fiends of the Infernal Pit': Joseph Smith's Incarceration in Richmond, Missouri, November 1838," *Mormon Historical Studies* 13, nos. 1–2 (Spring/Fall 2012):135–59.

3. For an examination of the Liberty Jail experience, see Dean C. Jessee, "'Walls, Grates, and Screeking Iron Doors': The Prison Experience of Mormon Leaders in Missouri, 1838–1839," in *New Views in Mormon History: A Collection of Essays in Honor of Leonard J. Arrington*, ed. Davis Bitton and Maureen Ursenbach Beecher (Salt Lake City: University of Utah Press, 1987), 19–42. In a hearing held on January 25, 1839, Judge Turnham released Rigdon, although he remained in jail for his own safety until February 5, 1839. See Richard S. Van Wagoner, *Sidney Rigdon: A Portrait of Religious Excess* (Salt Lake City: Signature Book, 1994), 254–55.

4. Hyrum Smith, Diary, April 1839, manuscript, 23, 26, Church History Library. Samuel Tillery, the jailer at Liberty who had overseen the four-month incarceration of the prisoners, was also in the company. Hyrum noted that "all these [men] were friendly & good natured." Before their transfer, there was some concern for the safety of the prisoners once they arrived in Gallatin, since the people there had considerable animosity toward and antagonism against the Mormons.

5. Peter H. Burnett, *An Old California Pioneer by Peter H. Burnett, First Governor of the State* (Oakland, CA: Biobooks, 1946), 39. In addition to Burnett and Rees, the Mormon prisoners also employed Alexander W. Doniphan as counsel. See Burnett, *Old California Pioneer*, 32. Doniphan had already argued much of the defense during the preliminary hearing at Richmond and during Sidney Rigdon's examination in January 1839. See Alexander W. Doniphan, "Interview," *Saints' Herald*, Aug. 2, 1884, 490.

6. Smith, Diary, 23–24.

7. Manuscript History of the Church, vol. C-1, 914; and *History of the Church*, 3:309.

8. Smith, Diary, 24–25.

9. Joseph Hedges McGee, "The Mormons in Missouri: Personal Recollections of Maj. Joseph H. McGee of Gallatin—Why the Mormons Were Forced to Leave the State," *St. Louis Globe Democrat*, November 27, 1898, n.p. McGee incorrectly identified Creekmore as "Crickmore." See also *History of Daviess County, Missouri: An Encyclopedia of Useful Information, and a Compendium of Actual Facts* (Kansas City: Birdsall & Dean, 1882), 249.

10. Alexander McRae to the Editor, Nov. 1, 1854, in "Incidents in the History of Joseph Smith," *Deseret News Weekly*, Nov. 9, 1854, 1.

11. Smith, Diary, 25.

12. Burnett, *Old California Pioneer*, 39.

13 Smith, Diary, 29. Speaking of their accommodations, Alexander McRae said, "We were seated at the first table with the judge, lawyers, &c., and had the best the country afforded; with feather beds to sleep on—a privilege we had not before enjoyed in all our imprisonment." McCrae, "Incidents in the History of Joseph Smith," 1.

14 Smith, Diary, 26.

15 Smith, Diary, 29.

16 Burnett, *Old California Pioneer*, 39.

17 Burnett, *Old California Pioneer*, 40–41. Joseph H. McGee is the source indicating that John Brassfield was the Prophet's wrestling opponent. He also reported that Joseph Smith threw Brassfield "the first two falls out of a match of three." See Joseph H. McGee, Statement, in "Some of the Waste Places of Zion as They Appear Today," *Deseret Evening News*, Sept. 10, 1904, 23. In 1888, assistant Church historian Andrew Jenson, along with Edward Partridge and Joseph S. Black, went on a historical fact-finding mission where, among other places, they visited numerous sites in northern Missouri. While visiting in Liberty, Clay County, they interviewed James H. Ford. In 1838–39, Ford was the deputy sheriff of the county. During the course of their interview, Ford shared with them additional details concerning the wrestling incident as recorded by Jenson: "[The Mormon prisoners] were handed over to some half-a-dozen of the strongest and roughest men of Daviess County, who at first crowded the prisoners into a corner of a room, refusing to allow them any liberties at all, but after a little, when they began to converse with the prisoners, they became quite sociable with them, and a reputed champion wrestler of Daviess County wanted to try [his] strength with the 'Mormon' Prophet. Joseph excused himself saying, he was a prisoner and could not engage [in] exercises of that kind under the circumstances; but finally, through the solicitations of the guard and the man promising not to get angry if he was thrown, Joseph consented to wrestle with him. Consequently a ring was made and the two stepped forth. The Missourian took recourse to all the trickery known to him in the art of wrestling, but was unsuccessful in his attempts to throw Joseph. Finally the latter gathered up his strength, made a first real attempt and threw his opponent flat upon his back in a pool of water. This made the fellow mad, although he had agreed not to get offended if thrown, and he wished to fight, but the guard interfered and the Daviess County champion was much humiliated afterwards in being made the object of considerable ridicule on the part of his companions, he having previously boasted that he could easily throw Joseph Smith." (Andrew Jenson, *Autobiography of Andrew Jenson, Assistant Historian of the Church of Jesus Christ of Latter-day Saints* [Salt Lake City: Deseret News Press, 1938], 164–65.)

18 Burnett, *Old California Pioneer*, 40. Lyman Wight gained the friendship of the guard by drinking with him. Burnett noted that Wight became "pretty well drunk, and would kindly invite the guards of Davis [sic] County . . . to drink with him, which invitation was cordially accepted" (Burnett, *Old California Pioneer*, 39).

19 Sidney Rigdon, Affidavit, in *Mormon Redress Petitions: Documents of the 1833–1838 Missouri Conflict*, ed. Clark V. Johnson (Provo, UT: Religious Studies Center, 1992), 679; *History of the Church*, 3:463. The Manuscript History of the Church and the published *History of the Church* both incorrectly state that the hearing was presided over by Austin A. King. See Manuscript History of the Church, vol. C-1, 914; and *History of the Church*, 3:309. Court records clearly indicate that Thomas Burch was the judge assigned to the case. Hyrum Smith's and Lyman Wight's affidavits also indicate Burch presided, not King. See Hyrum Smith, Affidavit, in *Mormon Redress Petitions*, 636; *History of the Church*, 3:421–22, 349; and Lyman Wight, Affidavit, in *Mormon Redress Petitions*, 664.

20 Josiah Morin also spent the night, and his presence lifted the spirits of the Mormon prisoners. Joseph Smith's manuscript history states: "We had as pleasant a time

as such circumstances would permit, for we were as happy as the happiest; the Spirit buoyed us above our trials, and we rejoiced in each other's society." Manuscript History of the Church, vol. C-1, 914; and *History of the Church*, 3:310.

21. The jurors included Robert P. Peniston (foreman), Nicholas Trosper, Benedict Weldon, John Stokes, Elijah Frost, Andrew McHaney, Christopher Stone, John Edwards, Moses Netherton, Jacob S. Rogers, Nathaniel Blakely, Jonathan Oxford, Richard Grant, Robert P. Peniston Sr., John Pinkerton, John Brown, William Cox, John Dowdy, John Anderson, and John Raglund. Proceedings of the Grand Jury of Daviess County, Apr. 2, 1839, Missouri, Boone County Circuit Court Records, Indictment Case No. 1362, folder 1, manuscript, 2, Joint Collection, University of Missouri and State Historical Society of Missouri, Ellis Library, Columbia, MO. The court document was originally filed in the Daviess County Court. However, because the prisoners received a change of venue to Boone County, the document became part of the Boone County Court record. The document is dated April 2, 1839, suggesting that the grand jury was appointed and preparations were already under way several days prior to the arrival of the Mormon prisoners.

22. Smith, Affidavit, 637; and *History of the Church*, 3:422.

23. Wight, Affidavit, 664; and *History of the Church*, 3:449.

24. Smith, Diary, 27.

25. Manuscript History of the Church, vol. C-1, 914.

26. Smith, Diary, 27–29.

27. A list of the Missourians that can be documented as having participated in the Hawn's Mill Massacre is found in Appendix I of Baugh, *A Call to Arms*, 203–11.

28. Smith, Diary, 30; Manuscript History of the Church, vol. C-1, 918–19; and *History of the Church*, 3:314–16.

29. Proceedings of the Grand Jury of Daviess County, 2.

30. Smith, Affidavit, 638; and *History of the Church*, 3:423.

31. Daviess County, Court Order, 1839, manuscript copy, L. Tom Perry Special Collections, Harold B. Lee Library, Brigham Young University, Provo, UT, hereafter cited as Perry Special Collections; Proceedings of the Grand Jury of Daviess County, 2. On April 9, 1839, the day the trial began, Stephen Markham arrived in Gallatin with a copy of a document from the state legislature authorizing the court to grant the prisoners a change of venue, which document was likely presented by the defense counsel to Burch for consideration. See Manuscript History of the Church, vol. C-1, 914.

32. The State of Missouri Order of Commitment—Caleb Baldwin and Others, manuscript copy, Perry Special Collections. The Manuscript History of the Church incorrectly identifies John Pope as John Pogue. See Manuscript History of the Church, vol. C-1, 914; and *History of the Church*, 3:309.

33. Smith, Diary, 30. Wight actually built two cabins at Di-ahman. The first was located about 1,200 feet west and south of present-day Tower Hill, and this is probably the cabin where they stayed. The cabin location is significant because this was where Joseph Smith likely recorded the revelation given on May 19, 1838, which comprises D&C 116, and where in June 1838 the Adam-ondi-Ahman Stake was created. A second cabin owned by Wight was situated about a hundred yards west of the top of Tower Hill.

34. Smith, Diary, 31.

35. Ibid.

36. Smith, Diary, 32. Hyrum Smith notes that Cox lived in Clinton County—an obvious error, since Clinton County is situated west of Caldwell County. He probably meant Livingston County.

37. Smith, Diary, 32.

38. Wight, Affidavit, 664; and *History of the Church*, 3:449.

39. Wight, Affidavit, 664. In an article that appeared in the *Columbia Patriot* (Columbia, MO), April 27, 1839, as cited in the *Missouri Republican* (St. Louis, MO), May 2, 1839, the report stated that the Mormons were released somewhere in Linn County. Lyman Wight stated that they were released at Yellow Creek, and although the creek passes through both Linn and Chariton counties, evidence suggests that the getaway took place in Chariton, not Linn County. In

a letter by William Barbee—writing from Carrollton, Missouri, to Thomas Bradford on April 22, less than a week after the incident—Barbee noted that the prisoners were released "about 12 miles north of this [place]," meaning twelve miles north of Carrollton, in Carroll County. See William Barbee to Thomas Bradford, Apr. 22, 1839, in "Expulsion of a Poor, Deluded and Miserable Set of Villains: A Contemporary Account," *Dialogue: A Journal of Mormon Thought* 11, no. 4 (Winter 1978):116. On a northeast line, Chariton County is approximately fourteen to fifteen miles from Carrollton, and Yellow Creek is just a few miles further distant. The point at which Yellow Creek is located in Linn County is at least forty miles from Carrollton.

40 The secondary sources that discuss the release of the Mormon prisoners generally give the date of April 15 because this is the date given in *History of the Church*, 3:320. However, the Manuscript History of the Church, Hyrum Smith's diary, and Lyman Wight's published history all indicate that the release occurred on the evening of April 16. See Manuscript History of the Church, vol. C-1, 921; Smith, Diary, 32; and Lyman Wight, "History of Lyman Wight," *Deseret News*, Aug. 25, 1858, 109.

41 Wight, Affidavit, 664; and *History of the Church*, 3:449.

42 Smith, Affidavit, 638; and *History of the Church*, 3:423.

43 Joseph Smith Jr., "Extract, from the Private Journal of Joseph Smith Jr.," *Times and Seasons*, November 1839, 7; Karen Lynn Davidson, David J. Whittaker, Mark Ashurst-McGee, and Richard L. Jensen, eds., *Histories, Volume 1: Joseph Smith Histories, 1832–1844*, vol. 1 of the Histories series of *The Joseph Smith Papers*, ed. Dean C. Jessee, Ronald K. Esplin, and Richard Lyman Bushman (Salt Lake City: Church Historian's Press, 2012), 483.

44 Smith, Affidavit, 638; and *History of the Church*, 3:423.

45 Smith, Diary, 32.

46 Joseph Smith, Diary, December 30, 1842, manuscript, Church History Library; as cited in Dean C. Jessee, "'Walls, Grates, and Screeking Iron Doors,'" 42n57.

47 Heber C. Kimball, *Heber C. Kimball's Journal*, in Faith Promoting Series (Salt Lake City: Juvenile Instructor Office, 1882), 73. Price later became a U.S. congressman, governor of Missouri, and a Confederate general. For an overview on Price's public career, see Rick Eiserman, "Sterling Price: Soldier—Politician—Missourian," in *Missouri Folk Heroes of the 19th Century*, ed. F. Mark McKiernan and Roger D. Launius (Independence, MO: Herald Publishing House, 1989), 115–34.

48 David White Rogers, Report, Feb. 1, 1839, manuscript, 2, Church History Library. Although the letter is dated February 1, Rogers made additional entries in the manuscript for several subsequent weeks.

49 Joseph H. McGee, *Story of the Grand River Country, 1821–1905: Memoirs of Maj. Joseph H. McGee* (Gallatin: North Missourian Press, 1909), 13; and McGee, *History of Daviess County, Missouri*, 206. There is an interesting side note to Bowman's death. On June 12, 1847, while camped at the North Platte River crossing near present-day Casper, Wyoming, Brigham Young's vanguard Mormon pioneer company met up with an overland group from Missouri. Someone in the Missouri company confirmed that William Bowman had indeed been killed for having let Joseph Smith and the prisoners go. Clayton learned that the person primarily responsible for Bowman's killing was William Obediah Jennings. Clayton referred to Jennings as Obediah, his middle name. See William Clayton, *William Clayton's Journal: A Daily Record of the Journey of the Original Company of "Mormon" Pioneers from Nauvoo, Illinois, to the Valley of the Great Salt Lake* (Salt Lake City: Deseret News), 233. In *An Intimate Chronicle: The Journals of William Clayton* (Salt Lake City: Signature Books, 1995), under the date of June 12, 1847, editor George D. Smith did not include the entry by Clayton about Bowman's death.

50 This conclusion is based on a statement by Joseph H. McGee, who wrote: "The court ordered Morgan to take the prisoners to Columbia and lodge them in jail, and

Morgan intrusted [sic] them to William Bowman." McGee, "The Mormons in Missouri," n.p.

51 William Morgan, Statement, The State of Missouri Order of Commitment, July 6, 1839, Perry Special Collections. Morgan's statement appears below the Order of Commitment, which is undated and unsigned and reads: "You will take their Recognizance for Five hundred dollars each."

52 McGee, *Story of the Grand River Country*, 13.

53 Parley P. Pratt to Mary Ann Pratt, Apr. 12, 1836, 1, Church History Library. The letter is dated April 12, but Pratt made additional entries under the dates of April 21 and 22. Although Pratt was concerned that the escape of Joseph Smith and his companions could have negative repercussions in connection with the upcoming trial of the Richmond prisoners, Judge King released two of the Mormon prisoners on April 24—Darwin Chase and Norman Shearer.

54 William Barbee to Thomas Bradford, in "Expulsion of a Poor, Deluded and Miserable Set of Villains," 116.

55 Samuel Bogart to the Quincy postmaster, Apr. 22, 1839, in Alexander L. Baugh, "Samuel Bogart's 1839 Letter about the Mormons to the Quincy Postmaster," *Nauvoo Journal* 7, no. 2 (Fall 1995):54.

56 Isaac J. Harvey to Sarah Harvey, April 26, 1839, 2, Perry Special Collections.

57 W. W. Phelps to Sally W. Phelps, May 1, 1839, as cited in Alexander L. Baugh, "A Community Abandoned: W. W. Phelps' 1839 Letter to Sally Waterman Phelps from Far West, Missouri," *Nauvoo Journal* 10, no. 2 (Fall 1998):26.

58 *Chicago Times*, Aug. 7, 1875, as cited in Jessee, "'Walls, Grates and Screeking Iron Doors,'" 41n56.

59 Rogers, Report, 2.

60 Smith, Affidavit, 638; and *History of the Church*, 3:423.

61 McGee, "The Mormons in Missouri," n.p.; and McGee, *Story of the Grand River Country*, 13.

62 Joseph Smith, Promissory note to John Brassfield, Apr. 16, 1839, photocopy in author's possession.

63 Kimball, *Heber C. Kimball's Journal*, 74.

64 Manuscript History of the Church, vol. D-1, 1684; and *History of the Church*, 5:290.

65 Joseph Smith III, "The Memoirs of President Joseph Smith (1832–1914)," ed. Mary Audentia Smith Anderson, *Saints' Herald*, November 13, 1934, 1454. Joseph H. McGee also recalled that sometime after the release of the Mormon prisoners, Brassfield traveled all the way to Nauvoo to secure the money from the note. See McGee, "The Mormons in Missouri," n.p.; and McGee, *Story of the Grand River Country*, 13. Significantly, in Lyman Wight's sworn statement given before the municipal court of Nauvoo in July 1843, he stated that at the time of their escape, part of the guard helped them mount their horses, "which we purchased of them, and for which they were paid." Wight, Affidavit, 664; *History of the Church*, 3:449. Wight's acknowledgment that "they were paid" may have had reference to Brassfield's visit to Nauvoo only five months earlier, during which time he received payment from Joseph Smith.

66 See William G. Hartley, "'Almost Too Intolerable A Burden': The Winter Exodus from Missouri," *Journal of Mormon History* 18, no. 2 (Fall 1992):7–40; Sean J. Cannon, "Expulsion from Missouri," in *Historical Atlas of Mormonism*, ed. S. Kent Brown, Donald Q. Cannon, and Richard H. Jackson (New York: Simon & Schuster), 48–49.

67 Smith, Diary, 33.

68 Such a course of travel possibly explains why Brigham Young and several members of the Twelve, who were traveling west from Quincy to Far West along the southern east-west route, did not meet up with Joseph Smith and his company, who were traveling east to Quincy across largely uninhabited prairie. Had the Prophet and his companions been taking the same main southern route as Brigham and the Twelve, they probably would have met each other.

69 Smith, Diary, 33–35. The individual referred to as George Harris by Hyrum Smith is not known, but he should not be confused with George W. Harris, who was a member of the Far West high council. Lyman Wight

identifies the Mormon man by the last name of Harrison. Lyman Wight, Journal, in Joseph Smith III and Heman C. Smith, *History of the Reorganized Church of Jesus Christ of Latter Day Saints*, 8 vols. (Independence, MO: Herald House, 1967), 2:330. The original Wight journal no longer exists. Hyrum Smith's diary appears to have been kept contemporaneously to the events as they happened, whereas portions of Wight's entries appear to have been added later; for that reason, Smith's journal is preferred over Wight's.

70 Manuscript History of the Church, vol. C-1, 924; and *History of the Church*, 3:327.

71 Orange L. Wight, Recollections of Orange L. Wight, Son of Lyman Wight to Joseph I. Earl, May 4, 1903, typescript, 7, Church History Library.

72 Wight, Journal, 330.

73 Ibid.

74 Dimick B. Huntington, Statement, as cited in David E. Miller and Della S. Miller, *Nauvoo: The City of Joseph* (Santa Barbara and Salt Lake City: Peregrine Smith, Inc., 1974), 26.

75 Manuscript History of the Church, vol. C-1, 924; and *History of the Church*, 3:327.

76 *Missouri Republican* (St. Louis, MO), May 3, 1839, 2.

77 Manuscript History of the Church, vol. C-1, 925; and *History of the Church*, 3:328.

78 John B. Clark, Interview, in Walter B. Stevens, *Centennial History of Missouri (The Center State): One Hundred Years in the Union, 1820–1921* (St. Louis and Chicago: S. J. Clarke, 1921), 119.

79 Smith, Affidavit, 635; and *History of the Church*, 3:420.

80 Gordon A. Madsen detailed the legal maneuvering of Judge King in the Richmond Court of Inquiry and concluded: "Austin A. King was determined to put Joseph and those he perceived to be principal Mormons in prison on some nonbailable charge and hold them there as hostages until the Mormons had all left the state." Gordon A. Madsen, "Joseph Smith and the Missouri Court of Inquiry: Austin A. King's Court of Inquiry," *BYU Studies* 43, no. 4 (2004):122. I came to this conclusion independent of Madsen in an earlier version of this narrative published in 2001, and gave additional evidence substantiating this point throughout the narrative. See Alexander L. Baugh, "'We Took Our Change of Venue to the State of Illinois': The Gallatin Hearing and the Escape of Joseph Smith and the Mormon Prisoners from Missouri, 1839," *Mormon Historical Studies 2*, no. 1 (Spring 2001):59–82.

81 Smith, Affidavit, 636; and *History of the Church*, 3:421.

82 Caleb Baldwin et al., Affidavit, in Johnson, *Mormon Redress Petitions*, 684–85. The names of Hyrum Smith, Caleb Baldwin, Alexander McRae, and Lyman Wight appear on the affidavit, but Joseph Smith's does not. The names of Parley P. Pratt, James Sloan, and Dimick B. Huntington also appear on the document. In June 1841, Missouri authorities attempted to arrest and extradite Joseph Smith on charges stemming from problems surrounding the 1838 Mormon-Missouri War and his so-called escape from the state. On June 4, 1841, an official from Missouri, assisted by several officials from Adams County, Illinois, arrested Joseph Smith. On June 10, following a three-day hearing at Monmouth, Warren County, Illinois, Judge Stephen A. Douglas dismissed the case and released the Prophet. See Manuscript History of the Church, vol. C-1, 1207; *History of the Church*, 4:370–71; George R. Gayler, "The Attempts of the State of Missouri to Extradite Joseph Smith, 1841–1843," *Northwest Missouri State College Studies* 19 (June 1, 1955):5–7; and *Missouri Historical Review* 58, no. 1 (Oct. 1963):24–26.

Mother and Father Smith
by Julie Rogers

Among the thousands of Mormon refugees seeking safety in Quincy were Joseph Smith Sr. and his wife, Lucy Mack Smith.

QUINCY

City of Refuge

by Susan Easton Black

Early Quincy residents compassionately cared for Mormon exiles from Missouri as one would care for an enduring friend,[1] expressing indignation at the Missouri governor's order proclaiming, "The Mormons must be treated as enemies, and must be exterminated or driven from the State."[2] Citizens of Quincy disregarded religious differences and embraced downcast Mormons crossing the Mississippi River; their solicitous reception during the winter of 1838–39 is unparalleled in the annals of Mormonism and has never been forgotten. It has become a legacy that epitomizes all that is good in people.

The story of this legacy begins just as Mormon founder Joseph Smith was concluding that the patriarch Abraham and the ancients would "not have whereof to boast over us [meaning his followers] in the day of judgment" and that the Latter-day Saints would "hold an even weight in the balance with them."[3] At this season of lamentation, the citizens of Quincy reached out to heal wounds, redress wrongs, and assist the sorrowful. The residents of Quincy offered hearth and home, sustenance, and even their possessions to provide much-needed relief to the Mormon exiles.

Public Square, Quincy, Ill.

In the winter of 1839, the residents of Quincy offered much-needed relief to the Mormon exiles from Missouri.

Quincy historian Phil Germann recalled the generosity of the Quincy Saints on a 1999 WGEM News broadcast. He remarked, "It was [one of] the greatest humanitarian gestures in the United States, since Quincy in the 1830s was not prepared to welcome strangers. Travel was difficult and health precarious." He viewed the generosity of the forebears of his city as "one of the most significant events in the history of the community."[4]

In the winter of 1838–39, thousands of religious exiles trekked nearly two hundred miles from Far West, Missouri, to the banks of the Mississippi River.[5] Brigham Young noted that this was not the first time Latter-day Saints had been forced to move: "We have, time and again, and again, been driven from our peaceful homes, and our women and children been obliged to exist on the prairies, in the forests, on the roads, and in tents, in the dead of winter, suffering all manner of hardships, even to death itself."[6]

By 1839 able Mormon exiles had reached the Mississippi, while the less-fit succumbed to privation and suffering and met untimely deaths. Among those able to reach the river were Elisha Groves, James Sloan, and Burr Riggs. Elisha Groves recalled the circumstances leading to his encampment near the river: "On 16 November 1838 Judge Vinson Smith and others came into [my] home and ordered myself and family to leave our possessions . . . within three days leave [Daviess] county or they would take our lives, for there was no Law to save us."[7] James Sloan likewise related his struggles, swearing "that his life was threatened, his property taken, and he was obliged to flee the state with his family, greatly to his disadvantage."[8] And Burr Riggs reported that "a mob of one hundred and fourteen armed men" threatened the life of him and his family and "followed us about six miles and [then] left us."[9]

Groves, Sloan, and Riggs were not atypical Mormons suffering from the government-sanctioned Extermination Order. They were representative of Mormons forced to abandon their possessions and flee from Missouri. As historian Germann recalled the circumstances of the Mormons' flight to safety, he spoke of the Extermination Order "being out of place in a country established on the principles of religious freedom. . . . The governor's quote 'nits make lice,' in reference to killing Mormon children, is unacceptable in any society."[10]

Yet, unacceptable as the order was, Mormons were forced to flee or face death. Most chose to flee from the governor's wrath in hopes of escaping further atrocities. Many of the exiles journeyed to the west bank of the Mississippi River

> It is reported that Missouri Governor Lilburn W. Boggs said, "Nits make lice"—a reference that seemingly sanctioned the killing of Mormon children.
>
> *Saints Driven from Jackson County Missouri* by C. C. A. Christensen

> By late winter of 1839, hundreds of Mormon exiles lined the banks of the Mississippi River.

and encamped directly across from Quincy, which was then home to sixteen hundred settlers—mostly natives of New England. It was not the settlers of Quincy, nor the agrarian possibilities of the community, nor even the picturesque setting of the city on the limestone bluff that prompted Mormons to gather across from Quincy. Among other things, it was the ferry boat facilities in Quincy Bay that attracted the exiles. They hoped the rivercraft would transport them out of Missouri to safety.

Unfortunately, floating ice delayed most rivercrafts from conveying the religious exiles to safety. The "ice had broken up on the west side of the river and was running so the ferry boat could not cross," wrote Sarah Rich. "All chance for crossing was to go across in a skiff or canoe through the ice until they reached the island and from there walk on the ice to reach Quincy on the east side," she continued.[11]

Under those conditions, most Mormons did not attempt to cross the treacherous waters. During February and March of 1839, hundreds waited anxiously for the river either to freeze completely or to melt and permit passage. With their scant provisions, most exiles huddled together in makeshift tents. Wandle Mace, a citizen of Quincy, wrote that "some had sheets stretched to make a little shelter from the wind, but it was a poor protection, the children were shivering around a fire which the wind blew about so it done them very little good. The poor Saints here suffered terribly."[12]

Among the refugees waiting to cross the icy river was Lucy Mack Smith, mother of the Mormon Prophet Joseph Smith. She wrote, "The snow was now six inches deep and still falling. We made our beds upon it and went to rest with what comfort we might under such circumstances. The next morning our beds were covered with snow and much of the bedding under which we lay was frozen. We rose and tried to light a fire, but, finding it impossible, we resigned ourselves to our comfortless situation."[13]

Some Mormons, anxious to escape further suffering, attempted to cross the river in canoes. "In the midst of great dangers," wrote Sarah Rich, "[they] crossed the river in a canoe,

Rescuers, by A. D. Shaw

The citizens of Quincy gathered food and supplies and risked their lives to ferry life-saving products across the Mississippi to the suffering Saints huddled together on the western bank of the river.

paddling through the ice, the women holding onto the side while the floating ice cut their fingers."[14] Not all who attempted the voyage were as fortunate. Martha Thomas recalled that on her voyage, "We made our landing good at Quincy, the other boat was surrounded with ice and taken out of sight, below town. I was much troubled for fear they would all be drowned."[15] Fortunately, her fears were not realized.

Others waited for a more opportune crossing, believing it to be when the river would soon freeze over. Yet how could they be sure at any point that the river was frozen enough to cross? As they waited, "the good people of Quincy" courageously boarded a canoe and pushed through the icy formations to bring needed relief. Wandle Mace wrote that the people of Quincy "donated liberally, the merchants vieing with each other as to which could be the most liberal. They soon had the contributions together, which filled a large canoe with flour, pork, coffee, sugar, boots, shoes and clothing, everything these poor outcasts so much needed."[16]

As the river froze, Mormons who had benefitted from the generosity of the people of Quincy crossed on the ice to Quincy—their city of refuge. One such young man was Mosiah Hancock, who recalled seeing "great blocks of frozen ice all over

Mosiah Hancock described the dangers of crossing the frozen Mississippi barefoot.

Run Mosiah
by Sandra Rast

the river, and it was slick and clear. . . . I being bare-footed and the ice so rough, I staggered all over. We finally got across, and we were so glad, for before we reached the other side, the river had started to swell and break up. Father said, 'Run, Mosiah,' and I did run! We all just made it on the opposite bank when the ice started to snap and pile up in great heaps, and the water broke through!"[17]

Another who reached safety was Emma Smith, the wife of Joseph Smith. With two babies (Alexander and Frederick) in her arms, and two children (Joseph and Julia) at her skirts, Emma walked across the frozen Mississippi seeking a place of refuge.[18]

Upon reaching land, many Mormon exiles could not refrain from expressing joy at

When the river finally froze, you get citizens of Quincy lining up on the bank telling the Saints and yelling across the river to send their children. So you get several waves crossing the river. The first will be the children. And Mosiah Hancock, a child at the time, writes that as he runs across he can hear from one side of the river, 'Go Mosiah!' and then from the other side, 'Come, Mosiah!' In other words, 'Get yourself across.'

"So the children went first to make sure that the ice was strong enough to support them, and then came the adults. And you'll notice that Emma Smith, she wouldn't send her children without her. So as she crosses that river she's got two babies in her arms, two children holding onto her skirts. She's got pockets sewn in her attire so she can carry across the manuscript of Joseph's Bible translation. And you see this huge sacrifice. As the people came across, it was estimated by those in Quincy that they were helping about 5,500 refugees from Missouri who were Latter-day Saints. For many of these refugees they were brought up to what was called—and still called today—Washington Park." —**Susan Easton Black**

their newfound freedom. Perhaps, as today, they saw the eagles flying overhead near the shoreline and remembered the guarantees of religious freedom contained in the U.S. Constitution.[19] Of the many who expressed joy, Parley P. Pratt perhaps best conveyed what these exiles felt. When he arrived in Quincy, "[Pratt] immediately stepped a few paces into the woods, and, kneeling down, kissed the ground as a land of liberty, and then poured out [his] soul in thanks to God."[20]

Pratt knew, as did another exile, Joseph Holbrook, that he had come "in[to] a land of freedom once more by the help of God and his blessings."[21] "Once more," Parley and fellow Mormons were "free to seek the pursuits of happiness and the welfare of the human race."[22] Lyman Littlefield wrote of the emotional greetings of "husbands and wives, parents and children . . . Brethren and sisters, of like precious faith."[23]

Yet, amid these joyous reunions, the Saints knew that their lives were still in peril. Hate-filled Missourians were crossing the Mississippi River and laying plans to kidnap unsuspecting Mormons. Such was the fate of Alanson Brown, James Allred, Benjamin Boyce, and Noah Rogers. These men were forcefully taken from Quincy across the Mississippi into Lewis County, Missouri. There Brown was hung from a tree until nearly strangled. Boyce was tied to a tree, stripped of his clothing,

Night Crossing
by Liz Lemon Swindle

With two babies in her arms and two children tugging at her shirts, Emma Smith walked across the frozen Mississippi to reach safety in Illinois.

Erastus Snow presented a series of lectures in the Quincy courthouse about Mormonism. His lectures did much to foster goodwill and compassion for the Mormons' plight.

and inhumanly beaten, as were Rogers and Allred.[24]

Not wishing the same fate, most of the displaced Mormons attempted to protect themselves from further atrocities. Their efforts would have been fruitless had it not been for the citizens of Quincy, who offered their uncompromising protection. Their only question seemed to be, "Why are Mormons so persecuted?" To answer their query, Erastus Snow presented a series of lectures in the Quincy courthouse about Mormonism. A biographer of Snow wrote of his lectures, "[At the courthouse] I first saw him, and wondered at his marvelous gift in explaining the Scriptures."[25] One author points out that ironically, while Quincy reverend George Moore—a graduate of the Harvard Divinity School—claimed to find these sermons "boring," he "never tired of writing about them."[26]

Whether profound or boring, the lectures of Erastus Snow and others led many of the people of Quincy to offer protection, food, and clothing to the religious exiles. Their unbounded generosity was not done in secret. Their kindness was extolled on both sides of the river. The adulation caused suffering Mormons, still entrapped in Missouri, to set their course for the Mississippi and then for Quincy. So many religious exiles came to Quincy that soon the refugees outnumbered the residents of Quincy by more than three to one. By April 1839, Quincy's homes were bulging with refugees, and makeshift tents covered Washington Park.[27]

Joseph Hovey, an eyewitness to the sprawling tents in the park, wrote of seeing Latter-day Saints "[with] nothing but the canopy of heaven to shelter them and many were sick. I had a feeling for their welfare and I remained and assisted my brother, Orlando, to administer medicine to the sick to the best of my knowledge and experience."²⁸ Wilford Woodruff wrote, "[I] saw a great many of the Saints, old and young, lying in the mud and water, in a rainstorm, without tent or covering. . . . The sight filled my eyes with tears."²⁹

Observer Wandle Mace offered his house to the suffering Mormons. "Many of the Saints were glad to find shelter in my house from the storms," wrote Mace. "Many nights the floors, upstairs and down, were covered with beds so closely it was impossible to set a foot anywhere without stepping upon someone's bed."³⁰

Quincyan Esaias Edwards also offered his house: "I found some of those unfortunate individuals camped out in the snow storm and I was filled with compassion towards them. And I told them if they would come home with me that I would receive them into my house."³¹

The kindness offered by Mace and Edwards was mirrored again and again by other citizens of Quincy. Lucy Mack Smith wrote of the "ladies of Quincy [sending] us every delicacy which the city afforded." Of special mention was the Messer family, of whom Lucy penned, "[They] sought every opportunity to oblige us while we remained in the place."³²

William Cahoon wrote of the Travis family offering employment.³³ Aroet Hale wrote of a Mr. Stilson employing his father.³⁴ And Luman Shirtliff wrote of arriving in Quincy in the evening hours and "wondering how we should get up the hill with our things, as weak as we were, and where we could stay overnight." He then noted, "When the boat landed many of the citizens came on board" to assist.³⁵ Thus, in a very caring manner, the citizens of Quincy assisted the exiled Saints.

The local Democratic Association of Quincy encouraged more assistance through a series of resolutions. In February 1839 the association

> Mormons flocking to Quincy outnumbered the citizenry of Quincy three to one. To even the casual observer, it appeared that every corner of the barn and living space was filled with refugees.

The John Wood Cabin Quincy, Illinois, by Kirt Harmon

Orville Browning, an attorney in Quincy, witnessed the suffering of the Latter-day Saints as they crossed the Mississippi. He was influential in encouraging the residents of Quincy to be compassionate to the Mormon refugees.

Orville Hickman Browning
by Brady Handy

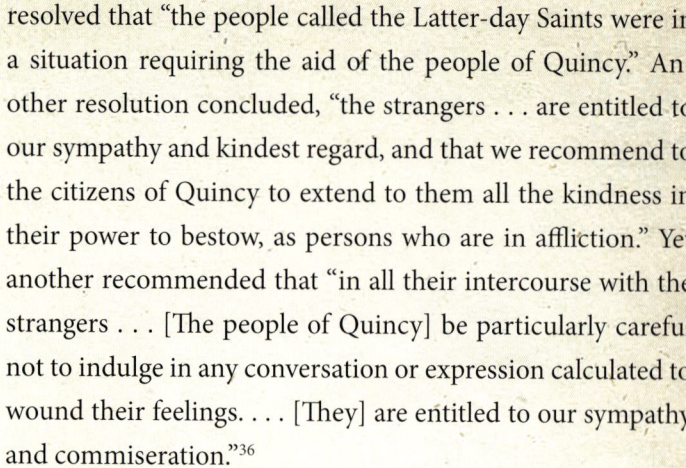

resolved that "the people called the Latter-day Saints were in a situation requiring the aid of the people of Quincy." Another resolution concluded, "the strangers . . . are entitled to our sympathy and kindest regard, and that we recommend to the citizens of Quincy to extend to them all the kindness in their power to bestow, as persons who are in affliction." Yet another recommended that "in all their intercourse with the strangers . . . [The people of Quincy] be particularly careful not to indulge in any conversation or expression calculated to wound their feelings. . . . [They] are entitled to our sympathy and commiseration."[36]

Encouraging these resolutions was famous Quincy lawyer Orville H. Browning. "Great God! have I not seen it?" said Browning. "Yes, my eyes have beheld the blood-stained traces of innocent women and children, in the drear winter, who had traveled hundreds of miles barefoot, through frost and snow, to seek a refuge from their savage pursuers."[37] His account of Mormon suffering was so moving that many who listened, including Judge Stephen A. Douglas and other community leaders, were in tears.

As more relief measures were adopted, the residents of Quincy were soon embarrassed to find themselves financially burdened by their own generosity. Seeking relief, yet wanting to keep benevolence at an appropriate level, they recommended that John Greene go east to raise additional "means to relieve the sufferings of this unfortunate people."[38] These and other extraordinary efforts to assist the downtrodden followers of Joseph Smith were in place when the Mormon Prophet arrived in Quincy on April 22, 1839. He immediately recognized and appreciated that "in our time of deep distress, [the people of Quincy] nobly came forward to our relief, and, like the good Samaritan, poured oil into our wounds, and contributed liberally to our necessities."[39]

Joseph in Liberty Jail by Robert T. Barrett

Joseph Smith was a prisoner in Liberty Jail when Latter-day Saint exiles crossed the frozen Mississippi to reach safety in Quincy. Joseph arrived in Quincy on April 22, 1839.

He, like other Mormons, was most grateful for the unprecedented help. Whether in the form of food, clothing, shelter, or employment, the hand of mercy was evident at every turn. Yet the time had come to move on—to establish homes of their own in what would become the city of Nauvoo.

For Mormons who remained in Quincy, leaders established a local organization of The Church of Jesus Christ of Latter-day Saints. They appointed Daniel Stanton as stake president and Stephen Jones and Quincy resident Ezra T. Benson as counselors. This organization proved unnecessary by 1841, for the Mormon population in Quincy was reduced to seventy-seven people.

Although the Quincy population of Mormons dwindled dramatically in the 1840s, interaction between Mormons and Quincyans remained notable. For example, in August 1843, an excursion boat from Nauvoo carried Joseph Smith and other Mormon leaders to Quincy as invited guests of Quincy mayor John Wood. The mayor met his guests at the boat landing and hosted

> In May 1839, Latter-day Saints moved from Quincy to the fledgling community of Commerce, later known as Nauvoo. About fifty miles now separated the Mormons from their friends in Quincy. Notable among those friends was Quincy mayor John Wood.

them at a dinner party, in which "Brother Joseph" was the "after-dinner entertainer." The people of Quincy who listened to his words were "loath to have him depart."[40]

The journal of Joseph Smith contains entries of his hosting residents of Quincy in Nauvoo: "Friday, July 14, 1843—I was visited by a number of gentlemen and ladies who had arrived from Quincy on a steamboat. They manifested kind feelings." Another entry reads, "Captain White, of Quincy, was at the Mansion last night, and this morning drank a toast saying, 'May Nauvoo become the empire seat of government!'"[41]

After the death of Joseph Smith, Church leaders maintained ties with the people of Quincy. Some appreciatively wrote of the "friendly disposition [shown by the people of Quincy] in establishing . . . peace at Nauvoo" during the difficult days that followed the death of the Mormon founder.[42] Of special mention in Mormon annals was John Wood, of whom it was said, "Throughout all their troubles . . . the saints found a consistent and strong friend in John Wood."[43]

These extraordinary acts of kindness by the citizens of Quincy have been spoken of by members of The Church of Jesus Christ of Latter-day Saints in congregations throughout the world for more than 175 years. Sincere gratitude in German, Spanish, Korean, and French may sound strange to some residents of Quincy today, but such expression has been and always will be found in Mormon circles. During this same period, according to the Quincy Visitor's Guide, those residing in Quincy have "counted [their] blessing and good fortunes, endured an occasioned flood or tornado, and settled [into a community known as] the Gem City of the Mississippi Valley."[44]

Yet it was a surprise for most of the forty thousand residents of Quincy when the NBC affiliate WGEM aired in July 1999 a three-part news series featuring "Quincyans opening up their heart and their doors to the Mormons in the 19th century." Commentator Ron Brown, with a backdrop that read, "Quincy—City of Hope," spoke of Quincy in 1839 as "having 1600 people and growing fast, but not fast enough to be prepared to accept 5600 Mormon refugees into their community." He nonetheless assured his listening audience that "Quincy answered the call" for relief.[45]

He then featured Mormons of the twentieth century who remembered the significance of Quincy's outreach. "The actions of the people of Quincy make me want to be like them," said a descendant of an early Mormon exile. Another interjected, "I want to put my arms around the people for what they did for my ancestors." Yet another asked, "What would the Mormons have done if the people in Quincy hadn't welcomed them into their town? . . . Nowhere else is there a town that opened their hearts to us as Quincy did."[46]

To further remember past kindnesses, a Quincy Heritage Celebration was held on July 24, 1999. More than fourteen hundred descendants of exiled Mormons came to Quincy. They represented the early Mormon families of Joseph Smith, Brigham Young, Heber Kimball, Ira Hinckley, and many more. In spite of the 100-degree temperature, the throng of descendants, attired like pioneers, were excited to be in Quincy.

The Memorial Bridge between Missouri and Quincy was officially closed to enable the descendants to reenact the crossing of the Mississippi by their ancestors 160 years earlier. Although in the 1830s crossing of the icy river was a somber event, the walk of the descendants across the bridge was anything but sad. Singing and music from bagpipes and harmonicas filled the hot summer air. When asked, "Why such merriment?" Frankie Barlow, a descendant of exile Israel Barlow, said, "I am grateful he made the sacrifice so I could have a happy life. I appreciate what those good souls [in

Surveying Nauvoo by Del Parson

Quincy] did." A Hinckley family descendant remarked, "It is a grand feeling and a grand sensation to be with such hospitable people." Television commentators editorialized, "Their ancestors came in poverty, yet look how happy their descendants are."[47] Singing "When the Saints Go Marching In" and "Come, Come Ye Saints," the descendants took joy in the simple act of walking across the bridge.

Joining hands with Mormon descendants in what was becoming a parade were descendants of old Quincy residents. One such man was Dr. Richard Allen, a descendant of Captain James Brown, the sheriff and justice of the peace in Quincy in 1839. Dr. Allen was so moved by his walk across the bridge that he expressed a desire to stop each Mormon and welcome him or her to town.

Perhaps the most touching scene in the parade was a ninety-three-year-old woman in a wheelchair. She emotionally spoke of touching the hand of her Mormon grandfather, who had found refuge in Quincy the winter of 1839. "I am grateful for Quincy," she said. "To think I have lived to be wheeled across the Mississippi. It is wonderful."[48]

Spectators lined the streets to watch the growing parade. Many wondered what all the excitement was about, as descendants shouted, "Thank you!" and shook hands with the unsuspecting. Although the expressions of the descendants were sincere and heartfelt, they paled in comparison to the sentiments of their ancestors.

Who today can match the expressions of gratitude uttered in 1839? Expressions such as—"[The people of Quincy] burst the chains of slavery and proclaimed us forever free!

> Latter-day Saints have remembered with profound gratitude the sacrifices of the citizenry of Quincy for their ancestors in 1839. The residents of Quincy have institutionalized that memory in well-placed monuments and a room in the Quincy Historical Society Museum, where the story of the Quincy rescue is told.

If you were to look through the annals of American history and try to find something parallel, where you could find a community of so few willing to help so many, Quincy stands alone. And because of that, Quincy must be remembered."

—*Susan Easton Black*

Mormon Room at Quincy Historical Society Museum.

. . . Quincy, our first noble city of refuge, when we came from the slaughter in Missouri with our garments stained with blood, should not be forgotten."[49] Yet, on July 5, 2002, in a continuing effort to remember with gratitude the residents of Quincy, the Mormon Tabernacle Choir performed a benefit concert to a sellout crowd of 2,200 in the Morrison Theater at the Quincy Junior High School. The expressed purpose of the concert was "to say thank you for kindness extended 163 years ago by the citizens of Quincy to Latter-day Saints fleeing religious persecution in the winter of 1839."

The proceeds of the concert—$75,000—were given to Quincy mayor Charles W. Scholz by President Gordon B. Hinckley for the Quincy Area Community Foundation. On that occasion, President Hinckley said, "We shall always be grateful for the kindness, the hospitality, with which your people met our people who were exiles from the state of Missouri."[50]

On June 18–19, 2008, when the Mississippi River threatened to flood the old downtown of Quincy, 130 Latter-day Saint missionaries joined in the sandbagging efforts. Quincy mayor Jong Spring said, "I cannot put into words, quite frankly, how much it meant to us to have members of the ministry group from the Latter-day Saints, the young and the old men and women, pitch in and help us like that."[51]

In July 2014, members of the Quincy wards wore "Helping Hands" yellow

Left, Tabernacle Choir performs to a capacity audience of 1,700 in Morrison Theater in Quincy, Ill. Proceeds from the concert were donated to a public charity. Below, President Hinckley, accompanied by Mayor Charles Scholz, at left, speaks during benefit.

Photos by Jeffrey D. Allred

Choir concert thanks Quincy for kindness

BY R. SCOTT LLOYD
Church News staff writer

QUINCY, ILL.

For 163 years, this city has been warmly remembered by the Church for the generosity of its citizens in sheltering oppressed Latter-day Saints who crossed the Mississippi River from Missouri. On June 28, the Church said thank you through a concert put on by the Mormon Tabernacle Choir.

An audience of 1,700 filled the Morrison Theater to capacity for the 90-minute program, the proceeds of which were donated to the Quincy Area Community Foundation, a public charity. The concert was co-sponsored with broadcasting station WGEM by the *Quincy Heard-Whig*, a newspaper that existed in 1839, when the beleaguered Church members were given refuge in the city.

"We come here as those who love and appreciate the city of Quincy, Ill.," President Gordon B. Hinckley declared to the audience during the program.

"In the annals of our Church, the city of Quincy and its citizens will always occupy a position of the highest esteem. We shall always be grateful for the kindness, the hospitality, the civility with which your people met our people who were exiles from the state of Missouri. When Gov. Boggs issued his infamous extermination order, our people were compelled to leave the state of Missouri. It's almost impossible to comprehend in this day and time that such a thing could occur. But the fact is it did occur, and they traveled across most of the state of Missouri seeking asylum, not knowing where to go or what to do. And the citizens of Quincy welcomed them, took them in, sheltered them for the winter which was all about them until they were able to find a place up the river in Nauvoo, where they established that beautiful city on the Mississippi."

President Hinckley said the choir's performance was an expression of appreciation to the community for what occurred, and as a further expression, the choir was contributing $75,000, the proceeds of the concert.

"I don't have the check with me," he said playfully, prompting appreciative laughter. "They already have it in the bank. And there it will become a corpus for great civic endeavors and the blessings of the people of this wondrous community, which we shall always hold in sweet remembrance."

Quincy Mayor Charles Scholz responded: "Mr. President, as our forefathers welcomed the saints in their time of need, we renew that welcome tonight, and we add to it our sincere gratitude and appreciation for your generosity and our congratulations on the completion of this beautiful and historic temple in Nauvoo."

The mayor noted that the logistics for the concert were handled by the sponsoring newspaper, "an institution that spans, like the bonds between the Church and this community, the 19th, 20th and 21st century."

That continuing good will seemed to be reflected in the responsiveness of the audience to the program of nearly a score of hymns, anthems, choral masterworks, and folk songs. With applause lasting more than a minute and a half, the audience demanded a double encore and gasped with delight when it was announced one of the closing selections would be the choir's signature tune, "Battle Hymn of the Republic."

At one point in the program, choir announcer Lloyd Newell asked members in the choir to stand who trace their ancestral roots through Nauvoo and Quincy. More than two thirds of the choir stood. "I count myself among them," Brother Newell said.

After an enthusiastically received performance of "Come, Come, Ye Saints," the announcer said: "We come to Quincy to remember and give thanks." Recounting the events of Church members being forced from Missouri, he quoted a March 1839 editorial in the *Quincy Whig* saying, "We hasten to invite the attention of the charitable and humane to [the Mormons'] destitute condition. Having been robbed of their all, in most instances, by their merciless oppressors in Missouri, they have been compelled to hurry out of the state."

"The benevolent people of Quincy responded with compassion and generosity," Brother Newell remarked. "Opening their hearts and homes, they helped the saints find shelter, food and jobs. They listened to reports from the leaders of the Church and passed resolutions condemning Missouri's treatment of the Mormons. They stood firmly for the right, rejecting a cultural and religious genocide."

He said the humanitarian gesture is "more than a footnote to the 172-year history of the Church.... It represents the finest in a tradition of American ideals.... Quincy bears a legacy of mercy that ripples down through the centuries, reminding us that the milk of human kindness is always more powerful than force or fury. Those who oppress and do evil, those who willfully hurt others and trod under foot basic human rights have their moment and they soon fade to oblivion. But those who show mercy are never forgotten."

A large display of articles and photos on the front page of the *Herald-Whig* the next day reflected the impact the concert had made in the city.

"I think that I can't remember an event like this where virtually everyone you saw or spoke to on the street was talking about it," said Mary Winters, assistant general manager of the newspaper, who worked with choir officers in arranging for the concert. "To think you could sit in your own hometown and listen to the Mormon Tabernacle Choir defies expression. I couldn't believe I was sitting in the place where I went to junior high school and hearing the choir sing."

Located in Quincy Junior High School, an immense city landmark built in the 1930s, the Morrison Theater has been refurbished in the last 20 years and is "close to acoustically perfect," she said. Still, it was necessary to bring in a portable air-conditioning system for the concert, because public schools are typically closed in the summer, when air conditioning is necessary.

Prior to the concert, Craig Jessop, musical director, other choir officers and Church representatives were feted at a reception, where a set of keys to the original Nauvoo Temple was displayed. The 16 hand-wrought keys have been in the possession of the Historical Society of Quincy and Adams County since the 1940s. The society received them from descendants of Artois Hamilton, owner of the Hamilton House Hotel in Carthage, Ill., where the bodies of Joseph and Hyrum Smith were prepared following the martyrdom to be sent back to Nauvoo for burial. Prior to the Latter-day Saints' exodus from Nauvoo in 1846, the keys were reportedly given to Mr. Hamilton by President Brigham Young in appreciation for the hotel owner's efforts.

E-mail: rscott@desnews.com

CHURCH NEWS ● WEEK ENDING JULY 6, 2002 — 5

President Gordon B. Hinckley and the Mormon Tabernacle Choir in Quincy, 2002. Photos, courtesy of *Church News*.

In 2002, President Gordon B. Hinckley brought the Mormon Tabernacle Choir to Quincy to perform a benefit concert. At the end of the concert, President Hinckley presented a check for $75,000 to the mayor of Quincy in appreciation for past kindnesses.

shirts as they cleaned up the downtown area. This was followed by a remembrance celebration in Washington Park and a performance by a dance company and jazz ensemble from Brigham Young University.[52]

Can the residents of Quincy expect more celebrations and expressions of remembrance? Absolutely! For there will always be those who remember the words of the Prophet Joseph Smith: "In our time of deep distress, [the people of Quincy] nobly came forward to our relief, and, like the good Samaritan, poured oil into our wounds, and contributed liberally to our necessities."[53]

Susan Easton Black

Susan Easton Black is an emeritus professor of Church History and Doctrine at Brigham Young University. She is a past Associate Dean of General Education and Honors and Director of Church History in the Religious Studies Center. Dr. Black has been the recipient of numerous academic awards for her research, including the Karl G. Maeser Distinguished Faculty Lecturer Award, the highest award given a professor at BYU. She has recently returned from serving a mission for the Church of Jesus Christ of Latter-day Saints.

ENDNOTES

1. Quincy was founded in 1825 and named in honor of newly elected U.S. president John Quincy Adams. The community is mentioned in the annals of history as the site of a senatorial debate between Senator Stephen A. Douglas and his less-known challenger, Abraham Lincoln. Quincy was the home of Orville H. Browning, a U.S. senator and secretary of the interior in President Andrew Johnson's cabinet. Quincy also claims such notables as Senator William A. Richardson and Illinois governors Thomas Carlin, Thomas Ford, and John Wood. *Quincy's Visitors Guide, 1999–2000* (Quincy, IL: Quincy Convention & Visitors Bureau, 1999).

2. James R. Clark, *Messages of the First Presidency of The Church of Jesus Christ of Latter Day Saints, 1822–1864* (Salt Lake City: Bookcraft, 1965), 3:46–47.

3. Joseph Fielding Smith, *Teachings of the Prophet Joseph Smith* (Salt Lake City: Deseret Book Company, 1961), 136.

4. "Quincy: A City of Hope," WGEM News—NBC Affiliate in Quincy, IL, July 21–23, 1999.

5. The distance from Far West, Missouri, to Quincy, Illinois, is about 150 miles in a straight line, but the way the roads ran in 1839 it was nearly 200 miles. Andrew Jenson, *Encyclopedic History of The Church of Jesus Christ of Latter-day Saints* (Salt Lake City: Deseret News Publishing, 1941), 688.

6. Brigham Young quote, in Henry Asbury, *Reminiscences of Quincy, Illinois: Containing Historical Events, Anecdotes, Matters Concerning Old Settlers and Old Times, Etc.* (Quincy, IL: D. Wilcox & Sons, Printers, 1882), 161.

7. Elisha H. Groves, in "History of Joseph Smith," *Millennial Star*, Oct. 13, 1855, 648; *History of the Church*, 4:68.

8. James Sloan, undated petitions, as cited in Clark V. Johnson, *Missouri Redress Petitions: Documents of 1833-1838 Missouri Conflict* (Provo, UT: BYU Religious Studies Center, 1992), 711.

9. Burr Riggs, in "History of Joseph Smith," *Millennial Star*, Oct. 13, 1855, 647; *History of the Church*, 4:67.

10. "Quincy: A City of Hope," WGEM.

11. Sarah Rich, Autobiography, 29–30, L. Tom Perry Special Collections.

12. Wandle Mace, Autobiography, 32–33, L. Tom Perry Special Collections.

13. Lucy Mack Smith, *History of Joseph Smith by his Mother* (Salt Lake City: Bookcraft, 1958), 296–97.

14. On March 4, 1839, days after her arrival in Quincy, Sarah Rich gave birth to a daughter. Andrew Jenson, *Latter-day Saint Biographical Encyclopedia* (Salt Lake City: Andrew Jenson History Company, 1901–35), 3:208.

15. Martha Thomas, Autobiography, in "Daniel Thomas Family History" (n.p., 1927), 27, L. Tom Perry Special Collections.

16. Mace, Autobiography, 32–33.

17. Mosiah Hancock, Autobiography, 17, L. Tom Perry Special Collections.

18. Emma and her children crossed the ice on February 15, 1839. See "Illinois City Still Friendly to the Church," *LDS Church News*, Feb. 18, 1989.

19. Near Lock and Dam 21, as many as two hundred eagles feed in the open water during the winter season. *Quincy Visitor's Guide*, 12.

20. Parley P. Pratt, *Autobiography of Parley P. Pratt* (Salt Lake City: Deseret Book, 1980), 278.

21. Joseph Holbrook, Autobiography, 47, L. Tom Perry Special Collections.

22. Lyman Littlefield, Reminiscences (1888), 110, L. Tom Perry Special Collections.

23. Littlefield, Reminiscences, 110.

24. Roberts, *Comprehensive History*, 2:51.

25. "Funeral of Erastus Snow," in *Collected Discourses Delivered by President Wilford Woodruff, His Two Counsellors, the Twelve Apostles, and Others* comp. Brian Stuy

(Burbank, CA: BHS Publishing, 1987), 1.

26 George Moore, Diary, as cited in Donald Q. Cannon, "Reverend George Moore Comments on Nauvoo, Mormons, and Joseph Smith," *Western Illinois Regional Studies* 5 (Spring 1982):7.

27 What the people in Quincy did for the Mormons would be comparable today to the residents of Quincy opening their doors to an influx of 170,000 refugees for five months.

28 Joseph Hovey, Autobiography, 15, L. Tom Perry Special Collections.

29 "Wilford Woodruff History, from His Own Pen" *Millennial Star*, May 20, 1865, 311.

30 Mace, Autobiography, 31–32.

31 Esaias Edwards, Autobiography, 14–15, L. Tom Perry Special Collections.

32 Lucy Mack Smith, History, 1845, 289; Joseph Smith Papers, Church History Library; *History of the Church*, 299–300.

33 William Cahoon, Autobiography, as cited in "Reynolds Cahoon and Sons" (1960), 87, in author's possession.

34 Aroet Hale, Autobiography, 6, L. Tom Perry Special Collections.

35 Luman Shirtliff, Autobiography, 43, L. Tom Perry Special Collections.

36 A few historians have concluded that a political advantage was sought through this action. *Quincy Argus*, Mar. 16, 1839; H. C. S., "Missouri Troubles," in *Journal of History*, ed. Heman C. Smith, Frederick M. Smith, and D. F. Lambert (Lamoni, IA: Board of Publication, Reorganized Church of Jesus Christ of Latter Day Saints, Jan. 1908), 439.

37 Manuscript History of the Church, vol. C-1, June 9, 1841; *History of the Church*, 4:368.

38 *Mormon Redress Petitions*, 6.

39 Of special mention were "Governor Carlin, Judge Young, General Leech, Judge Ralston, Rev. Mr. Young, Col. Henry, N. Bushnell, John Wood, J. N. Morris, S. M. Bartlett, Samuel Holmes, and J. T. Holmes, Esquires, . . . whose kindness, on that occasion, is indelibly engraved on the tablets of our hearts in golden letters of love." First Presidency, "Proclamation to the Saints Scattered Abroad, Jan. 15, 1841," in *History of the Church*, 4:267.

40 Mary Ann Winters, "Account," in *Young Woman's Journal* 16 (Dec. 1905):557.

41 *New York Sun*, Sept. 4, 1843; "History of Joseph Smith," *Millennial Star*, Oct. 27, 1860, 684.

42 "Public Meeting," *Times and Seasons*, July 1, 1844, 566.

43 *Deseret News*, Sept., 1869; Brigham H. Roberts, "History of the Mormon Church," in *Americana* (New York: The National Americana Society), 598.

44 Quincy was recognized with the All-American City Award, 1962–1963 and again in 1984–1985 (see *Quincy Visitor's Guide*).

45 "Quincy: A City of Hope," WGEM.

46 Comments made by Sister Sagers, Robert King, and Rees Johnson, missionaries for The Church of Jesus Christ of Latter-day Saints serving in Nauvoo, Illinois.

47 "Quincy: A City of Hope," WGEM.

48 "Quincy: A City of Hope," WGEM.

49 John C. Bennett, "Inaugural Address, Feb. 3, 1841," in *History of the Church*, 4:292.

50 "Quincy," *LDS Church News*, July 2002.

51 "Historic Help Remembered in Sandbagging Effort," *LDS Church News*, Sept. 2008.

52 Program from the July 2014 Quincy "Helping Hands" celebration, in author's possession.

53 Of special mention were "Governor Carlin, Judge Young, General Leech, Judge Ralston, Rev. Mr. Young, Col. Henry, N. Bushnell, John Wood, J. N. Morris, S. M. Bartlett, Samuel Holmes, and J. T. Holmes, Esquires, . . . whose kindness, on that occasion, is indelibly engraved on the tablets of our hearts in golden letters of love." First Presidency, "Proclamation to the Saints," in *History of the Church*, 4:267.

Flight from Missouri by Julie Rogers

By March 1839, hundreds of Mormon refugees lined the western bank of the Mississippi River, seeking asylum in Illinois.

QUINCY

the Home of Our Adoption

by Richard E. Bennett

The Mormons—We hasten to invite the attention of the charitable and humane, to the destitute condition of some of this people. A large number of families are encamped on the opposite bank of the Mississippi, waiting for an opportunity to cross, who are, we understand, almost without common necessities of life. Having been robbed of their all in most instances, by their merciless oppressors in Missouri, they have been compelled to hurry out of the state.... They are certainly objects of charity and their privations and sufferings must call forth the sympathies of the humane and liberal. If they have been thrown upon our shores destitute, through the oppressive people of Missouri, common humanity must oblige us to aid and relieve them all in our power.[1]

So wrote the editors of the *Quincy Whig* in early March 1839 as the first of thousands of ill-treated Latter-day Saint refugees came into sight of their Illinois refuge. Banned and banished from their Missouri homes and properties in Caldwell and Daviess counties—some two hundred miles to the west—and with

Suffering Children
by A. D. Shaw

The Mormons were religious refugees in the true sense—they were robbed of their possessions and vilified by false reports for their religious beliefs.

their Prophet-leader Joseph Smith incarcerated in Liberty Jail, the Latter-day Saints (Mormons) were now in a pell-mell rush to quit Missouri by 8 March, the deadline set by Missouri Governor Lilburn W. Boggs, or face forced expulsion and extermination. Nothing like this attempt at religious genocide exists elsewhere in American history. And seldom has a city shown such relief, compassion, and genuine humanitarian concern as did the citizens of Quincy in those dark days of 1839.

This chapter explores the essential elements and characteristics of the relatively short but extremely important Mormon stay in Quincy and its environs between the intermittent arrival of the Mormons in February of 1839 and their piecemeal departure for Commerce (later to become Nauvoo) beginning some four months later. Considering the fact that Quincy played the lead role of refuge and relief to a hunted and hurried people, a humanitarian lifeline in a sea of turmoil, it is more than a little surprising that so little serious research has been devoted to the topic. While much has been written in Church history about the Mormon stay in Missouri and even more about their experience in Nauvoo, Quincy is relatively understudied. One reason for such a deficit may lie in the fact that the written accounts are relatively few. As one weary traveler put it, after November 1838 "our troubles were so numerous that I could not and did not write any more while we were driven out of the state."[2]

The tragic Mormon expulsion from Missouri is well known and needs little rehearsal here.[3] Suffice it to say that in the dead of winter, several thousand Mormon settlers-turned-refugees were in a desperate search for some place—any place—to live and find shelter for that winter of 1838–1839. "We left Far West Missouri 10 January," Albert P. Rockwood recorded,

. . . with another family and arrived at the Mississippi River after a journey of twelve days, the distance of 200 miles. We had snow and rain every day but we had heavy loads and were obliged to walk from 2 to 8 miles a day through mud and water. Camped out on the wet ground 3 nights before we arrived at the [Mississippi] River. A few days before we got to the river it grew cold, the river froze over and we were obliged to camp close to the river for 3 days.[4]

William Hickman likewise tells of "much suffering and distress amongst those who were leaving Missouri, women and children barefooted and hungry."[5]

Reflecting on the tragedy of it all and wondering who might befriend them—and why—James Stapleton Lewis recorded these forlorn sentiments:

When we get to another state how shall we be received? My outfit was sorry enough but what can the people say to us? Here is a family exiled and driven out of Missouri as unfit to live in that sovereign state. Can we look anybody in the face, can we expect a favor or even a kind look from anybody not only so but Missouri sent all her influence against us word with all manner of false and slanderous reports against us.[6]

One reason the Latter-day Saints fled to Quincy was its geographic location on the Mississippi River.

John Wood Mansion in Quincy

Samuel H. Smith, The First Missionary by William Whitaker

In 1831, Samuel H. Smith, the brother of the Prophet Joseph Smith, preached in Quincy.

Why Quincy?

The immediate question is *why Quincy?* The answers are multiple and complex, and while some are obvious, others require elaboration. The obvious first answer is geographic. Under government decree, the Mormons had to quit the entire state of Missouri, ruling out a river retreat to St. Louis or some other eastern towns in that state. A return to Kirtland, Ohio, the former Mormon capital, was impossible. The only answer could be somewhere close and somewhere safe.

Quincy, with an 1839 population of approximately 1,800 and a distance of some 200 miles away, was the largest and closest Illinois city to Mormon properties in western Missouri. Furthermore, as the county seat of the newly formed Adams County, it could well serve as the base for making legal petitions for redress to be carried to Missouri's capital in Springfield, which was approximately 200 miles away.

A second answer is economic. By 1838, Quincy was well on its way to an economic boom. E. B. Kimball had just established a wonderful new flour mill. S. B. Stoddard and C. Maertz were opening their stove-making facility. C. Appleton and

Company were newly into the wagon and carriage business, and A. Jones was just beginning to sell his successful steel plows. Besides these establishments, Quincy could boast its share of coopers and cabinet-makers, saddlers and leather-makers, and a pork-packing and meat-processing center that rivaled any other city on the Mississippi north of St. Louis. It was a city on the move, destined to double in size to 4,400 by 1840 and then to mushroom to 30,000 just ten years later. Surrounded by some of the richest farmland in the West, the "Gem City" was looking for workers and rich new opportunities.[7]

A third answer is familiarity. Mormon missionaries first preached in the city with the arrival of Samuel H. Smith, who was on his way to Jackson County in 1831.[8] Early Mormon settlers bound for Missouri stopped off at Quincy in 1832.[9] Zebedee Coltrin was preaching in Quincy in February 1834. Later known as Zion's Camp, the quasi-military expedition sent out from Kirtland, Ohio, to alleviate the suffering of Mormon settlers in Independence, Missouri, had passed through Quincy in the summer of 1834 (or at least that portion from Michigan led by Hyrum Smith and Lyman Wight), stopping to purchase lead and ammunition. They described the town then as a "considerable place containing about 70 houses, two inns, nine stores, and an open square in the center."[10] And by 1838, there were scores of

> In the summer of 1834, a contingency of Zion's Camp journeyed through Quincy on their way to Clay County, Missouri.
>
> *Zion's Camp March*
> by T. B. H. Stenhouse

> Quincy was not only a place of refuge for Mormons, it was also a station on the Underground Railroad for slaves who were seeking freedom.

Latter-day Saints already living in the city—members like Mary Jane York, William A. Hickman, John P. Greene, and Wandle Mace, some of whom had resided there since at least 1835.[11]

More to the point, the Latter-day Saints had already drunk from Quincy's milk of human kindness. Back in 1832, James Lewis had been taken sick while en route west "but was cared for in all kindness and soon recovered in Quincy."[12] While traveling to Missouri in 1838, John P. Greene (a cousin by marriage to Brigham Young and Heber C. Kimball), "came to Quincy and put up at Judge Cleveland." Greene described Cleveland as "a very fine feeling man and benevolent to all and who ministers to the necessities of the afflicted Saints."[13] In fact, as a Quincy inn keeper, Greene formed friendships with several prominent merchants and professionals in the city to raise funds to aid the Latter-day Saints, and it was he who strongly encouraged Brigham Young and the Saints in exile to come to Quincy.[14]

Even by this time Quincy, with its strong German and New England population base, had developed a reputation as a center for intellectual inquiry, equality, and humanitarian care and relief. The City Library was established in 1837. Quincy was also a station on the Underground Railway for Black slaves in search of freedom.[15]

Finally, there was the hope of new lands for the Saints to settle near Quincy at very reasonable rates. From the minutes of a conference of the Church held at Quincy in early 1839, we read that "John P. Greene by request, told of an offer made by a gentleman of 20,000 acres of land lying between the Mississippi and Des Moines River at $2 an acre to be paid in 20 installments without interest. A committee had looked at the land and reported favorably."[16] Isaac Galland of Commerce had purchased land north of the city on both sides of the river and was anxious to find buyers among the Latter-day Saints.[17]

For these reasons, as well as for the hope for decent medical care and adequate schooling, from five to seven thousand Latter-day Saints struggled across Missouri in the general direction of Quincy.

The Underground Railroad
by Charles T. Webber

Like the Good Samaritan: Quincy Opens Its Doors

By the time of their arrival on the banks of the Mississippi, the Mormons were indeed a sorry-looking, destitute people with no other options than to cross the river—itself no small ordeal. "When we came to the Mississippi River," Samuel Gifford recalled, "Father who opened his own rented home to some of the refugees and some others cut down two very large cottonwood trees and dug them out in the shape of canoes and lashed them together a sufficient distance apart to admit the wheels of wagons in which many of the Saints crossed the river, steering their craft between the large cakes of ice that were then floating in the river, while the smaller cakes would pass between the two canoes."[18]

Wandle Mace, a Mormon living in Quincy, provides this sobering snapshot:

> One cold blustery morning I went down to the riverside and found about fourteen or fifteen families camped on the river bottom, in a most miserable condition; they had crossed the river (one boat at a time) and would get no further. Some of them had tried to make a little shelter from the wind, by placing some polls [sic] in the ground and placing a sheet over them. The wind was

Taking them In
by Julie Rogers

blowing the snow about them so that the poor children who was [sic] hovering over a little fire trying to get a little warmth received very little benefit from it. I returned as soon as possible and made know there [sic] situation and in a very short time they were moved into town and made comfortable.[19]

Although Quincy Mormons such as Sidney Rigdon (recently released from Liberty Jail), John P. Greene, and Wandle Mace were doing all in their power to alleviate the suffering of their fellow Saints, it was generally the city residents who came willingly to the rescue of the Mormons and made the vital difference. During the late Mormon difficulties in Missouri, Quincy had taken a wait-and-see (though rather sympathetic) stance toward the Saints. "We are well aware that the hostility is more deeply seated than has been generally supposed," reported one writer of the Quincy Whig in November 1838, "and we feel assured that bloodshed and devastation only will terminate the struggles, unless the Mormons remove from the County. . . . We hope to be able to develop shortly more of the causes of this unhappy state of affairs."[20]

A month later, the same newspaper reported on "the distress of these people, without home or shelter of any kind," and concluded, "A heavy sin lies somewhere and between the leaders of this misguided sect and the Missourians, it is difficult to fix the responsibility."[21]

Soon after Sidney Rigdon's release from Liberty Jail and his arrival in Quincy in mid-February to promote the plight of his people, in a way perhaps only the outspoken and passionate Rigdon could inspire, public sentiment had clearly shifted. "The celebrated Mormon preacher and leader, Sidney Rigdon, arrived in Quincy on Saturday at last," reported the Quincy Whig on February 23, 1839.

> *Illinois at present appears to be an asylum to the oppressed people as they are coming from all quarters. They appear, so far as we have seen, to be a mild, inoffensive people who would not have given a cause for the persecutions they have met with; and the whole proceedings of this people by the authorities of Missouri must stand as a lasting stigma to the State."*

Sidney Rigdon was released from Liberty Jail earlier than the other Mormon prisoners because of illness. He arrived in Quincy in mid-February 1839, two months before the Prophet Joseph and his brother Hyrum arrived.

Two nights later, in what Wandle Mace referred to as local "merchants vieing with each other as to which would be most liberal," the Democratic Association of Quincy drew up measures of relief for the recent newcomers. Long-time local merchant Mr. Lindsay "introduced a resolution setting forth that the people called the 'Latter-day Saints' were many of them in a situation requiring the aid of the citizens of Quincy and recommending that measures be adopted for their relief."[22]

The list of other prominent Quincy citizens, both Whig and Democrat, who came out in support reads like a "Who's Who" of Quincy, Illinois, in 1839. It includes such prominent names as Samuel and J. T. Holmes, merchants; I. N. Morris, attorney at law; J.W. Whitney; Thomas Carlin, governor of Illinois; Richard M. Young, U. S. Senator; Samuel Leech; Hiram Rogers, M.D.; Nicholas Wren, county clerk; C.M. Woods; and John Wood, Quincy's mayor and earliest citizen.[23] By Thursday, February 28, Holmes, Whitney, and Wood had collected $73 from town leaders to donate to the Mormons.[24]

It is difficult to ascertain to what degree the townspeople were motivated politically and economically by the sudden arrival of thousands of potential new voters, still smarting from Democrat Governor Boggs's Extermination Order. There were certainly political overtones. Nevertheless, the alarming spectacle of so many newcomers knew no party or persuasion. Mr. N. Bushnell, a prominent local attorney, "disclaimed in strong terms against the pitiful interests of the Democratic Association in taking solely upon themselves the care and protection of the Mormons. He said he never could nor should contribute in aid of this suffering people,

In 1839 Governor Thomas Carlin was among the citizens of Quincy who supported humanitarian efforts to assist the Mormon refugees.

as a member of the 'D.A.', but as a citizen of Quincy."²⁵

Several public appeals for assistance went out from such meetings and discussions.²⁶ The response was truly immediate and gratifying in terms of financial assistance, shelter, and employment. "The people of Quincy have contributed between $400 and $500 dollars," reported Israel Barlow. "God has opened their hearts to receive us. May heaven's blessings rest upon them. We are hungry, they fed us, naked, they clothed us. The citizens have assisted us beyond calculation."²⁷

The most immediate need of the refugees was for shelter. Isaac Galland opened up at least a dozen of his small cabins by the river to accommodate the Saints. Several other Saints stayed at "the old Methodist Institute" five miles out of town.²⁸ Joseph Smith's parents, Joseph Smith Sr. and Lucy Mack Smith, rented a house (or a part of it) on the northeast corner of Sixth and Hampshire, where for a short time they "set up a museum of curiosities, consisting mainly of several mummies from Egypt."²⁹ John L. Butler recalled that there was one old man, whose name he had forgotten, who:

Israel Barlow said of the residents of Quincy, "We are hungry, they fed us, naked, they clothed us. The citizens have assisted us beyond calculation."

> kept a large butcher shop down by the river and a large wholesale store down by the boat landing. He also had ten or twelve small houses that he had built on purpose to rent. He told some of his tenants that they had to seek other apartments for the Mormons were coming and they had no place to go and he was going to give his apartments to them. So the old gentlemen came to me and told me to bring my family up to one of his houses and we could live in it till we had been there a little while, so that we should have a little time to look about us and get a place. He also told us to go down to the butcher's store and get some meat when we wanted some. He never charged us anything for what we had. There were three or four other families living close to us that were Mormons; they were living in his house that was joining ours. He treated them all with kindness. It seemed a new thing to us to be treated with kindness. . . . The folks generally were kind to our brethren all over the place.³⁰

Many others were taken in by local townsfolk and nursed back to health. It was all enough for one woman to later write, "I don't feel afraid, me dear friend, if you should come here that you would not like our little city . . . the home of our adoption."[31]

As for employment, local historian Henry Asbury noted that "many found temporary employment in Quincy,"[32] whether in sawmills or on steamboats, stagecoach driving or railroad building, blacksmithing or tanning, keeping school or sewing bonnets. One bit of Quincy misfortune turned out to be a blessing in disguise. Fire destroyed the meat-packing plant of Harrison, Rice, and Ward on Tuesday, March 26, 1839. Many Mormons were put to work rebuilding destroyed parts of the plant; and though the building was saved, much of the meat had to be sold at a greatly reduced price—a godsend for the Saints.[33]

Quincy's timely aid and humanitarian assistance will be forever remembered in Mormon history. "The inhabitants of Quincy were very kind to us as a people," remembered Sarah Pea Rich, "and done all they could to give our brethren employment and assisted many that were in need and many who were sick."[34] William Cahoon told of Quincy as a place "where we found a people who treated us with the greatest of hospitality and kindness assisting the Saints with food and given them houses to live in. . . . I went to live with a man of the name of Travis who gave me employment and linaments and my bosom burns with gratitude."[35] Another writer, Samuel K. Gifford, recalls the citizens of Quincy donating "quite freely to help the most destitute of the Saints. Such will be remembered when it is said 'Inasmuch as you have done it unto the least of these my servants, you have done it unto me.'"[36]

Perhaps the following 1841 proclamation of Joseph Smith, Hyrum Smith, and Sidney Rigdon best epitomized the Mormon expression of appreciation:

Sarah Pea Rich recalled that the people of Quincy not only gave food and shelter to the Latter-day Saints, but also provided employment.

> *It would be impossible to enumerate all those who in our time of deep distress, nobly came forward to our relief and like the good Samaritan poured oil into our wounds and contributed liberally to our necessities as the citizens of Quincy en masse and the people of Illinois generally seemed to emulate each other in the labor of love.*[37]

Not everyone was filled with gratitude, however. Some were willing to take whatever they could get, despite the living or the dead. Take the case of a Mr. Robert Stilson and his haunted house. Anxious to rent his vacant farmhouse to the newest tenants, Stilson willingly rented out his property to Mormon newcomer Mr. Hale and his young family. So long as Hale did not mind living in a spooked environment, Stilson would repay Hale—and then some—for every improvement he made such as painting, fencing, and so on. The story was that a Black peddler had been murdered there and his body thrown into the well. Hale, a very active Latter-day Saint, saw absolutely no problem with the arrangement since he, as a priesthood holder, could cast out every devil in Adams County. Just don't tell the wife! And so, on a smile and a handshake, Hale took residency.

All went well for several months, until one dark night.

> *Father had called the family together for prayers at bed time and had read a chapter in the Book of Mormon and had knelt down and commenced to pray when there was something that fell on to the top of the house that fairly shook the house so that the dishes rattled on the cupboard . . . and so Father sprang to his feet run to the door up the corner of the house on to the roof and rebuked the evil spirits and commanded them to depart. Came back, knelt down and had his family prayers. A few Sundays after this occurrence, Father was having prayers before going to bed. He was on his knees and had commenced praying when there was something sounded like a man braying and a lot of log chains past [sic] by close to the door. These logs [had lain] for a week in front of the door. The chains rattled over those logs and passed to the end of the house. Father sprang to his feet ran down to the door and commenced rebuking this evil spirit and commanded it to depart and leave the premises. It started off dragging its chains. He followed it about 20 rods, returned to the house, had prayers and went to bed.*
>
> *The third and last time was on Sunday again at the close of the meeting. We had had a very good meeting. The Spirit of the Lord had been in our midst to*

a great degree. One of the sisters looked across the room and there stood the Devil or evil spirit in the shape of a large Newfoundland dog only much larger with eyes glaring like balls of fire looking into the house. This scared the women and children. Father spoke to one of the Brethren [and] they followed this spirit off of the farm and into the woods rebuking it by the power of the Priesthood and ordered it to return no more. No more evil spirits returned to bother us.[38]

Scattered About

A city so small as Quincy, despite its every good intention, could not begin to meet the needs of so many. Nor was it the Mormon design to relocate en masse in any new central location. While John P. Greene and others were out scouting the Galland properties for what eventually did become Nauvoo, Presiding Bishop Edward Partridge thought that in light of their recent Missouri difficulties, "it was not expedient under the present circumstances to collect together, but thought it was better to scatter into different parts and provide for the poor."[39]

Consequently, the Saints scattered hither and thither into numerous small communities and farmlands within a fifty- to seventy-five-mile radius of Quincy. Hale found his haunted house near New Liberty, just east of Quincy. Quite a large number of Saints, finding "all the houses were full" in Quincy, moved to the northern part of Adams County and set up shop at Bear Creek Timber (Woods) near Lima, some twenty miles north.[40] Headed up by Isaac Morley, the so-called Morley Settlement was arguably the largest concentration of Mormons outside of Quincy. First a branch and then, for a short time, a stake of the Church, the Morley Settlement featured, among other things, a thriving home-chair-building industry. "I stayed in the Morley Branch to learn the chair trade," recalled Samuel Gifford, and "labored at chairs the most of the time the Saints remained in Illinois. . . . In October [1848] Father Whiting

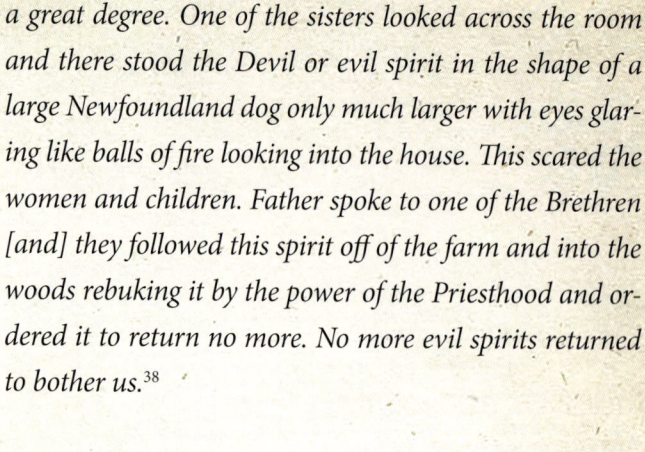

In the winter of 1839, negotiations began with Isaac Galland, a land speculator, to acquire large tracts of land about fifty miles upriver.

The largest concentration of Latter-day Saints outside of Quincy lived in the Morley Settlement, named after founder Isaac Morley. The settlement was later known as Yelrom, which is Morley spelled backward.

was fixing to go to Quincy, Illinois, where we had a regular market for our chairs."[41]

Warren Foote and several other families took refuge on farmland near Columbus, some fifteen miles east of Quincy. Getting a job as a stagecoach driver, Foote drove the run from Columbus to Naples, a distance of forty-five miles. His choice of rest and relaxation may not have been unusual for the time.

> There was an old bachelor [in Belmont] boarding with the family I boarded with, and also a young man about my age. We had a sitting room to ourselves. The bachelor was a fiddler and we used to have considerable fun during the long winter evenings. The Methodists had a wonderful revival of religion in this neighborhood and we often attended their meetings to see their performances. It was as good to us as a theater.[42]

Martin Henderson rented John Gault's place near Rock Creek, some eight miles north of Quincy.[43] Ira Ames found shelter in "the little town of Clayton," where "several other Mormon families" lived.[44] James Allred settled in Pittsfield, Pike County,[45] and Lorenzo Young located in Macedonia.[46] There is even evidence that some were living as far away as Clinton, Illinois. The list could go on and on. Suffice it to say that the Mormons were scattered over hill and dale in Adams and surrounding counties; however, as many as possible chose to live close to Quincy because of the need for medical care, better schooling, and the desire to stay close to kin.

Renting farmland was (for most, anyway) the only hope for survival—and the area was known to be excellent for agriculture. "This is a good country here," admitted David Foote in a spring 1839 letter. "A man [has] no need to work half as hard in this country to get a living as you do to the east. Wheat is worth $1 and corn

$.25 per bushel, potatoes $.75, butter can be got for $.12 ½ per pound. We live 12 miles east of Quincy in the house with uncle Josiah Richardson."⁴⁷

Martin Henderson spent the winter cutting cord wood for a Mr. Simpson Bicky "at 50 cents per cord and took my pay in corn and pork. . . . Worked a part of the farm on which we lived, raised 18 acres of corn and sold the same."⁴⁸ Aroet Hale spent his winters catching quail and prairie chickens. "I have sent into Quincy 20 dozen quails and 150 chickens at a time. They was [sic] a good sale and brought the money into the family."⁴⁹ And by choosing to live near Quincy, when things slowed on the farm, there was always hope for work in town. "I returned to Quincy," recalled Edward Stevenson, "and found work at a steam sawmill for $.50 a day . . . wheel[ing] away saw dust and chop[ping] up slabs for $.50 a cord so between the two jobs I cleared double wage. But the work was hard for me."⁵⁰

Edward Stevenson was employed at a steam sawmill in Quincy. He chopped up slabs and hauled away sawdust.

Other Important Events in Church History at Quincy

This same Edward Stevenson tells of the Quincy refugees receiving letters from the Prophet Joseph Smith, then languishing in Liberty Jail, "believing that that God who seeth us in this solitary place, will hear our prayers and reward you openly."⁵¹ By April 1839, Joseph Smith, his brother Hyrum, and others were released from their incarceration and made a direct line for Quincy, arriving there April 21, 1839, "amid the congratulations of his friends and fond embrace of his family."⁵² "The celebrated Mormon leader, Joseph Smith, who has been in confinement in the upper part of Missouri, arrived in town on Monday last [April 22]," the *Quincy Whig* reported.⁵³

The Prophet's arrival electrified his followers, who for almost six months had wandered "as sheep without a shepherd."

Joseph and Emma by A. D. Shaw.

Upon finding his mother, father, wife, and children well, he took time to thank the citizens of Quincy. "I have been delivered out of their hands [referring to the Missourians]," he said, "and can enjoy the society of the Saints whom I love and to whom I feel united in bonds that are stronger than death; and in a state where I believe the laws are respected and whose citizens are humane and charitable."[54]

Speaking at an outdoor conference on May 4 held at the "old Presbyterian campground," Joseph made an unforgettable impression on those who heard him speak. "He stood for an unusual length of time without uttering a word," one observer remembered.

The Quincy Whig reported that Joseph arrived in town on April 21, 1839, "amid the congratulations of his friends and fond embrace of his family."

> His soul was filled with emotion and it seemed as though relief could not be uttered only with a flood of tears. He looked calm, however. . . . He then said, "To look over this congregation of Latter-day Saints who have been driven from their homes and still in good faith as pilgrims in a strange land, and to realize that my life has been spared to behold your faces again seemed to me so great a pleasure."[55]

Brigham Young functioned as the senior member of the Twelve in Quincy though he would not be set apart as president of the Quorum of the Twelve Apostles until April 1840, in Nauvoo.

Relying on intelligence and earlier reports from his subordinates, Joseph Smith at this same conference counseled the Saints to prepare to leave for Commerce and other nearby areas in the newly obtained Galland Purchase, what would soon become the city of Nauvoo, Illinois.

This Quincy conference was of more import than deciding on a new home. Several of the Quorum of the Twelve Apostles—some newly called and others sick—left on their memorable missions to England from this same Quincy area. And it was here that Brigham Young was set apart as the new president of the Quorum of the Twelve and where George A. Smith and Wilford Woodruff were sustained in their apostolic callings. Frederick G. Williams, a once-prominent leader in the Church and medical doctor by profession who at one time practiced in Quincy, was excommunicated (along with several others) only to rejoin the Church a few months later, shortly before his death.[56]

It was also in Quincy that Sidney Rigdon gathered up hundreds, if not thousands, of petitions for redress to be considered by both the U.S. government and the government of Missouri—petitions that fell largely on deaf ears.[57]

Little known in Church history is the fact that a Quincy branch of more than two hundred members was organized in 1840 with a Brother Calhoun presiding, and a short-lived Quincy stake was organized in October 1840 with Daniel Stanton as president.[58] In November 1840, for a very brief time, some members of the Quincy Branch—including the newly converted Ezra T. Benson—performed baptisms for the dead (presumably in the Mississippi River) until instructed to desist until further instruction was received and a proper baptismal font could be erected in the new Nauvoo Temple. This was among the very first instances of this sacred ordinance ever being performed in this dispensation.[59]

In August 1843, Quincy mayor John Wood, ever a friend of the Mormons, invited the Prophet and some of the leading citizens of Nauvoo to be his guests for the day. As one noted, "Brother Joseph was the after-dinner entertainer, for he talked and the others listened with the greatest attention and were loath to have him depart."[60] Within a year, the Mormon leader was dead, a victim of a vicious mob attack in Carthage, Illinois.

By 1848, Joseph L. Heywood, a former Nauvoo trustee following the exodus of the Mormons under Brigham Young in 1846, led a company of his own, comprising what may have been the last remnants of a Latter-day Saint population in Quincy, on a trek to the Great Basin. Not until 1949—more than a century later—would the Church return to Quincy, with Thomas Kinrade becoming the first Latter-day Saint branch president of this century in Quincy.[61] Today Quincy boasts two flourishing wards of the Church.

And they are put up in homes and in farms and in barrooms and in taverns and in livery stables throughout the whole city in February and March of 1839. The city transforms itself into a refugee capital. I don't think there's anything like it in American history. I don't think that any city of its size ever opened its homes and its kitchens and its farms and its places to welcome in a despised people that were three times the population of the city itself, as Quincy does in the winter of 1839. I don't know of any story in American history that comes close to it. —*Richard Bennett*

As one steps back into the clear light of historical evaluation, the meaning of the story of Quincy and the Mormons in 1839 far transcends a humanitarian gesture of goodwill to a peculiar band of religionists. To Mormon history, Quincy's compassion was a lesson in Christian service that saved the Saints and may have even saved the Church as a people and an institution.

Yet, in a very real sense, this merits far more than a footnote in either a Churchwide or local story. I like to think it represents the finest tradition in American history—a victory for that kind of tolerance, human kindness, and compassion that has welcomed millions of immigrants and huddled masses to its shores in previous centuries, as well as hundreds of thousands of refugees from Kosovo to Cambodia in modern times. Such openness and willingness to accept new culture, religionists, skin colors, and tongues has made America the great nation it is today.

Finally, on another level, the Quincy model is a lesson for all mankind. Extermination orders and cultural genocide, holocausts still exist, if not abound. Hatred and prejudices are ingrained in so many countries and cultural identities. Many people today are shivering on the banks of their own Mississippi Rivers all over the world, waiting and hoping to cross into a new and kinder world of improved attitudes and depressed prejudices. Will there be a Quincy in men's hearts for them? God make it so.

Richard E. Bennett

Richard Bennett has been an associate Dean of Religious Instruction at Brigham Young University and currently serves as the Chair of the department of Church History and Doctrine at Brigham Young University. He is a past president of the Mormon History Association, and is the author of numerous books and articles on LDS Church history. He was born and raised in Ontario, Canada, and is married to the former Patricia Dyer. They have five children.

ENDNOTES

1. *Quincy Whig*, Mar. 2, 1839.

2. Josiah Smith, Journal, Nov. 29, 1838, Church History Library.

3. For an excellent study of the Mormon expulsion from Missouri, see William G. Hartley, "'Almost Too Intolerable a Burthen': The Winter Exodus from Missouri 1838–1839," *Journal of Mormon History* 18, no. 2 (Fall 1992):6–40.

4. Letter of Albert P. Rockwood to his father, Quincy, IL, 1839, in Albert P. Rockwood Journal, Oct. 1838–Jan. 1839, Church History Library.

5. William A. Hickman, Autobiography, Church History Library.

6. James Stapleton Lewis, Autobiography, Church History Library.

7. Harry L. Wilkey, "Infant Industries in Illinois as Illustrated in Quincy, 1836–1856," *Journal of the Illinois State Historical Society* 32, no. 4 (Dec. 1939):474–97.

8. Lucy Mack Smith, *The Revised and Enhanced History of Joseph Smith by His Mother*, ed. Scot Facer Proctor and Maurine Jensen Proctor (Salt Lake City: Bookcraft, 1996), 280.

9. James Stapleton Lewis, Journal, book 2, 18, Church History Library.

10. Taken from the 1834 entries of the "Manuscript History of Illinois," an unpublished scrapbook-like collection, Church History Library. For a fuller discussion of the travels of Zion's Camp, see Roger D. Launius, *Zion's Camp—Expedition to Missouri, 1834* (Independence, MO: Herald Publishing House, 1984).

11. Mary Jane Bethers York, Biography, Church History Library.

12. Lewis, Journal, May 1832, book 2, 18.

13. John P. Greene, Diary, Nov. 15, 1838, Church History Library.

14. See John P. Greene, "Expulsion of the Mormons" (Cincinnati: R. P. Brooks, 1839), 6. Levi W. Richards wrote on February 12, 1839, "The people are preparing to leave as fast as they can conveniently. Many have already left. Our kindred are in Illinois and have been for weeks except cousin Brigham Young and his family, and they expect to start the day after tomorrow. I think I shall accompany them to Quincy and then return here (Far West) again for my goods, which will take about three weeks. Cousin Greene's family are in Quincy keeping Tavern." Journal History, Feb. 12, 1839.

15. See Paul R. Anderson, "Quincy, an Outpost of Philosophy," *Journal of the Illinois State Historical Society* 15, no. 3 (1922–23):579

16. Journal History, Feb. 1839.

17. Isaac Galland had been introduced to the Mormon plight by Israel Barlow. See Journal History, Feb. 26, 1839.

18. Samuel K. Gifford, Autobiography, Church History Library. Fortunately for the Latter-day Saints, the winter of 1838–39 had been unusually mild, which accounts for the earlier-than-normal breakup of river ice. An arrival four years earlier, when the temperature had reached minus thirty-two degrees Fahrenheit in January 1835, would have spelled an untold disaster. See Asbury, *Reminiscences of Quincy, Illinois*, 75; *Quincy Whig*, Jan. 19, 1839; *Quincy Whig*, Mar. 9, 1839.

19. Wandle Mace, Autobiography, 32, Church History Library. "Many of the Saints were glad to find shelter in my home from the storms," Mace continued, "until they could find a place to live in. Many nights the floors upstairs and down were covered with beds so closely it was impossible to set foot anywhere without stepping on some one's bed."

20. *Quincy Whig*, Nov. 10, 1838.

21. *Quincy Whig*, Dec. 22, 1838.

22. Journal History, Feb. 25, 1839.

23. Theodore C. Pease, *The Centennial History of the State of Illinois 1818–1848* (Springfield, IL: Illinois Centennial Commission, 1918), 343.

24. *Quincy Whig*, Mar. 16, 1839.

25. *Quincy Whig*, March 2, 1839. Bushnell went on to say "that the meeting [of the Democratic Association] was unknown to the great mass of the people of Quincy and that his object was solely of a charitable nature."

26 See opening quotation of this article.

27 Israel Barlow to his wife, Elizabeth, Feb. 24, 1839, as quoted in Ova H. Barlow, *The Israel Barlow Story and Mormon Mores* (The Israel Barlow Family Association, 1968), 150.

28 Sarah D. Pea Rich, Autobiography, Church History Library.

29 Asbury, *Reminiscences of Quincy, Illinois*, 153.

30 John L. Butler, "A History of the Biography of John L. Butler," 27–28, L. Tom Perry Special Collections.

31 Letters of Mary R. Heywood to Miss Sarah M. Blodgett, Oct. 13, 1840, and Apr. 3, 1841, in Papers of Joseph L. Heywood, Church History Library.

32 Asbury, *Reminiscences of Quincy, Illinois*, 153.

33 *Quincy Whig*, Mar. 30, 1839; see also Aroet Hale, Journal, Church History Library.

34 Rich, Autobiography, Church History Library.

35 William Farrington Cahoon, Journal, 47, Church History Library.

36 Gifford, Autobiography, 4.

37 "A Proclamation to the Saints Scattered Abroad—Greeting," *Times and Seasons*, Jan. 15, 1841.

38 Hale, Journal.

39 Minutes of a Church conference held at Quincy, IL, Feb. 1839, in Journal History, Feb. 1839.

40 "A Brief History of Almira Pulsipher Burgess," in Nora Hall Lund, *Pulsipher Family History Book* (1952), L. Tom Perry Special Collections.

41 Gifford, Autobiography, 4. He continued in the chair-making business while crossing the plains. "I stayed in Mt. Pisgah [Iowa] and worked in the chair shop until the fall of 1848."

42 Warren Foote, Autobiography, 45, Church History Library.

43 Martin Henderson, Memorandum, Church History Library.

44 Ira Ames, Journal, Church History Library.

45 James T. Allred, Biographical Sketch, Church History Library.

46 Lorenzo Young, Autobiography, Church History Library.

47 Letter of David Foote to his brother and sister, May 15, 1839, David Foote Collection, Church History Library.

48 Henderson, Memorandum.

49 Hale, Journal.

50 Edward Stevenson, Diary, 133, Church History Library.

51 Stevenson, Diary, 120.

52 Stevenson, Diary, 123.

53 *Quincy Whig*, Apr. 27, 1839.

54 Stevenson, Diary, 123. For more on Joseph Smith's gratitude to the citizens of Quincy and more especially to George Miller for providing for his family, see the author's article, "A Samaritan Had Passed By: George Miller—Mormon Bishop, Trailblazer, and Brigham Young Antagonist," *Illinois Historical Journal* 82 (Spring 1989):2–16.

55 Stevenson, Diary, 129.

56 Frederick Granger Williams, Autobiography, Apr. 6–7, 1840, Church History Library. Frederick G. Williams is buried in Quincy, IL.

57 *Mormon Redress Petitions: Documents of the 1833-1838 Missouri Conflict*, ed. Clark V. Johnson. Volume Sixteen in the Religious Studies Center Monograph Series. (Provo: Religious Studies Center, Brigham Young University, 1992).

58 See "A Record of The Branch of The Church of Jesus Christ of Latter-day Saints in Quincy, Illinois," Church History Library; see also "Manuscript History of the Quincy Branch, Northern States Mission," Church History Library. The Quincy Stake existed until the spring of 1841, at which time all stakes outside of Nauvoo, Illinois, and Lee County, Iowa, were discontinued.

59 See "A Record of the Branch in Quincy," Nov. 9 and 15, 1840; see also Roberts, *Comprehensive History*, 2:76, 92. Roberts indicates that Joseph Smith first taught the doctrine of baptism for the dead—an ordinance Mormons believe is one of conditional salvation for deceased ancestors—as early as 1840 and that some baptisms for the dead were performed in the Mississippi River until a baptismal font could be erected. He is silent, however, as to the location of such ordinances.

60 Mary Ann Winters, Account, in *Young Woman's Journal* 16, no. 12 (Dec. 1905):558.

61 LaPreel D. Huber, "A Brief History of the Church of Jesus Christ of Latter-day Saints in Quincy, Illinois, 1838 to 1969," 1, Church History Library.

Night Crossing
by Liz Lemon Swindle

Joseph Smith III described in some detail crossing the ice of the Mississippi River with his mother, Emma, and his siblings Julia, Frederick. and Alexander.

In Golden LETTERS OF LOVE

The Kindness of the Citizens of Quincy

by Lachlan Mackay

In the State of Illinois we found an asylum, and were kindly welcomed. . . . It would be impossible to enumerate all those who, in our time of deep distress, nobly came forward to our relief, and, like the good Samaritan, poured oil into our wounds, and contributed liberally to our necessities, and the citizens of Quincy en masse, and the people of Illinois, generally, seemed to emulate each other in this labor of love. We would, however, make honorable mention of Governor [Thomas] Carlin, Judge [Richard M.] Young, General [Samuel] Leech, Judge [James] Ralston, Rev. Mr. Young, Col. Henry, N[ehemiah] Bushnell, John Wood, [Isaac] N. Morris, S[ylvester] M. Bartlett, Samuel Holmes, and J. T. Holmes, Esquires, who will long be remembered by a grateful community, for their philanthropy to a suffering people, and whose kindness, on that occasion is indelibly engraved on the tablets of our hearts in golden letters of love.[1] —**Times and Seasons, Jan. 15, 1841**

Following the Battle of Crooked River, Governor Lilburn Boggs's Extermination Order, the Hawn's Mill Massacre, and the siege and surrender of Far West, members of The Church of Jesus Christ of Latter-day Saints slowly began turning their teams and wagons to the east. Most delayed their departure following the surrender of November 1, 1838,[2] hoping that Governor Lilburn W. Boggs's Extermination Order would be recognized as unconstitutional and they would be allowed to stay in Missouri.

By late January 1839, it was becoming clear that staying was not an option. Latter-day Saints pooled resources and worked together to help those in need flee from persecution. The journey out of Missouri was most difficult for the wives of those killed or injured in the war, as well as for the wives of Church leaders imprisoned following the conflict. Among the latter was Emma Hale Smith, wife of Joseph Smith Jr.

Their son Joseph Smith III recalls the family's exodus from Missouri in his memoirs:

> *We had an early start next morning, but of other incidents connected with the long journey of crossing the*

For Father and Mother Smith, the journey to Quincy was fraught with many struggles. Father Smith suffered much from a severe cough and the incessant rain.

Mother and Father Smith
by Julie Rogers

State I have little memory until we reached the river. The weather had become extremely cold and the river was frozen over, so that we crossed upon the ice. Charlie, the more intelligent animal of the team, was hitched to the tongue of the wagon and the driver, walking behind him, held the end of the tongue in his hand, guiding the horse across. This was considered the safest way to make the crossing for it was feared the ice might not be strong enough to bear the weight of the double team and the loaded wagon.

Carrying in her arms my brothers, Frederick and Alexander (the latter born the preceding June), with my sister, Julia, and myself holding onto her dress at either side, my mother walked across the frozen river and reached the Illinois shore in safety. This, then, was the manner of our passing out of the jurisdiction of a hostile State into the friendlier shelter of the State of Illinois, early in 1839.[3]

Joseph Smith Jr.'s parents, Joseph Sr. and Lucy Mack Smith, fled Far West, Missouri, with the help of their youngest son, Don Carlos Smith, as well as other family members. Even though the Smiths left many of their provisions and most of their furniture behind, the journey across northern Missouri to Quincy took them seven days. With a heavily loaded wagon and their horses in poor health, Lucy and Joseph Sr., who was ill himself, had to get out of the wagon and walk up every hill.[4]

By day two of the journey, Lucy was walking more than half the time and Joseph was "suffering much with a severe cough."[5] On day three, it began to rain. They found lodging that night in a farmer's outbuilding "filthy enough to sicken the stomach," with no wood for a fire, and were charged 75 cents for the privilege of staying there. The bone-chilling rain continued on day four as they traveled through the mud until near nightfall. They were refused shelter again and again before finding a filthy, unheated barn much like the one in which they had spent the previous evening.[6]

Day five found the weary travelers in Palmyra, Missouri. With the rain still falling, Don Carlos realized the family could go no further, and he declared that he would approach the next farmhouse and plead for help. In speaking to the landlord of the farmhouse, Don Carlos said:

"I do not know but I am trespassing, but I have with me an aged father, who is sick, besides my mother, and a number of women, with small children. We have travelled two days and a half in this rain, if we are compelled to go much further, we shall all of us die. If you will allow us to stay with you over

night, we will pay you almost any price for our accommodations."

"Why what do you mean, sir," said the gentleman, "Do you not consider us human beings? Do you think that we would turn anything that is flesh and blood from our door, in such a time as this! Drive up to the house and help your wife and children out: I'll attend to your father and mother and the rest of them."[7]

The landlord then helped the strangers into his home; hung up their soaked clothing to dry; provided food, water, and milk for the children; and provided the family with comfortable beds. Their host, it turned out, was a member of the Missouri House of Representatives.[8]

Worried about being trapped in Missouri by rising water, the Smiths pushed on through the rain the next morning. As they approached the Mississippi River, rain turned to hail and snow. The horses gave out; all the refugees were on foot, and with every step they sank ankle-deep in mud, occasionally stopping to search for shoes that had been sucked off their feet.[9]

Once at the river, they had no way to cross, and the snow

The Smiths waited patiently with the throngs of Latter-day Saints until nearly sunset before being ferried across the Mississippi River to Quincy.

The Story of the Great March
by George Ward Nichols

was six inches deep and still falling. They could find no shelter, for the shore was crowded with Latter-day Saints fleeing Missouri. The family made their beds on the ground and awoke covered with snow; only "after considerable pains" did they succeed in folding their frozen bedding. Unable to start a fire, they waited patiently until nearly sunset before being ferried across the river.[10]

The Smiths' son Samuel had secured a house in Quincy, so Lucy and Joseph Sr. moved in, making a total of six families in the home (according to Lucy).[11] Samuel told his parents the story of his exodus from Missouri. He and those traveling with him were saved from near starvation by a Native American woman who, although short of food herself, shared her wheat cakes with the hungry travelers, giving them the strength to continue their flight to Quincy.[12]

It was not until Lucy Mack Smith arrived in Quincy that she became very ill. She wrote of a pain that "almost burst the bones themselves asunder."

The Smiths soon found out what kind of people the residents of Quincy were. According to Lucy Mack Smith:

> We had many kind neighbors in fact they were all kind one in particular I would mention who lived across the street from us by the name of Messer this man and his wife seemed to seek every opertunity [sic] to oblige us and while we were there they took care that we were accommodated with everything that we needed which was at their command.[13]

Mother Smith went on to say that her daughter Lucy was stricken with what they believed to be cholera within a week of their arrival in Quincy and wouldn't eat. Mother Smith was soon sick herself with a pain that she described as "almost bursting the bones themselves asunder." A local botanic physician was brought in and he prescribed an herb tea. The pain was relieved immediately, and Lucy began to recover.[14] Again according to Lucy Mack Smith:

> During our sickness the ladies of Quincy sent us every delicacy which could be obtained with the hopes of pleasing our appetites particularly Lucy's [her daughter] as she was not inclined to take any kind of food into her stomach.[15]

Others besides Lucy Mack Smith also wrote of the kindness of the sixteen hundred Quincy citizens who gave comfort to refugees approximately three times their number.[16] In a letter to Joseph Smith Jr. and others confined in Liberty Jail, Edward Partridge wrote on March 5, 1839:

> The people receive us kindly here, they have contributed near $100 cash [a number that would soon grow much higher] besides other property for the relief of the suffering among our people. . . . The ice has run these three days past so that there has been no crossing, the weather is now moderating and the crossing will soon commence again.
>
> This place is full of our people, yet they are scattering off nearly all the while. . . . It is a general time of health here, We greatly desire to see you, and to have you enjoy your freedom. The Citizens here are willing that we should enjoy the privileges guaranteed to all civil people without molestation.[17]

Emma Smith, staying at a farm east of Quincy, wrote to Joseph two days later:

> Dear Husband
>
> We are all well at present, except Fredrick [their son] who is quite sick.
>
> Little Alexander [also a son of theirs] who is now in my arms is one of the finest little fellows, you ever saw in your life, he is so strong that with the assistance of a chair he will run all round the room.
>
> I am now living at Judge [John] Cleveland's four miles from the village of Quincy. I do not know how long I shall stay here. . . .
>
> The daily sufferings of our brethren in travelling and camping out nights, and those on the other side of the river would beggar the most lively description.

In a letter to her husband, Joseph, Emma penned, "The people in this state are very kind indeed, they are doing much more than we ever anticipated they would."

Portrait of Emma Smith by Lee Greene Richards

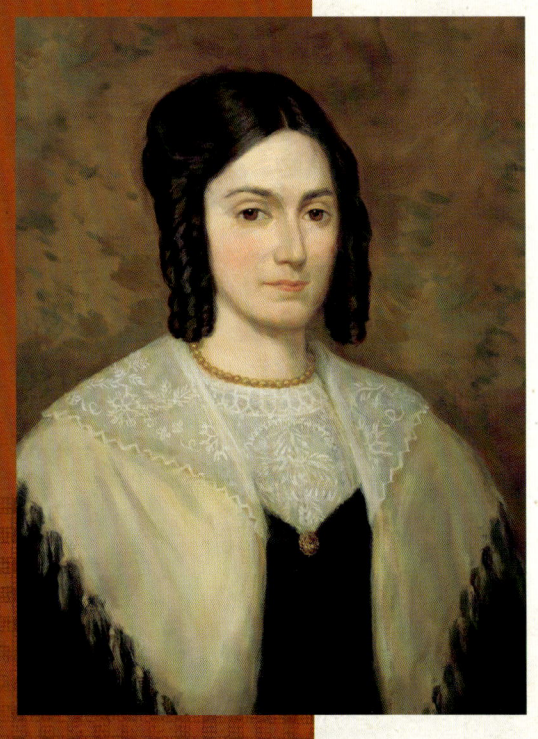

Quincy March 7th—

Dear Husband

Having an opportunity to send by a friend I make an attempt to write, but I shall not attempt to write my feelings altogether, for the situation in which you are, the walls, bars, and bolts, rolling rivers, running streams, rising hills, sinking vallies and spreading prairies that separate us, and the cruel injustice that first cast you into prison and still holds you there, with many other considerations, places my feelings far beyond description. Were it not for conscious innocence, and the direct interposition of divine mercy, I am very sure I never should have been able to have endured the scenes of suffering that I have passed through, since what is called the Militia, came into Far West, under the ever to be remembered Governor's notable order; an order fraught with as much wickedness as ignorance and as much ignorance as was ever contained in an article of that length; but I still live and am yet willing to suffer more if it is the will of kind Heaven, that I should for your sake.

We are all well at present, except Friedrich who is quite sick. Little Alexander who is now in my arms is one of the finest little fellows, you ever saw in your life, he is so strong that with the assistance of a chair he will run all round the room. I am now living at Judge Cleveland's four miles from the village of Quincy. I do not know how long I shall stay here. I want you to write an answer by the bearer. I left your change of clothes with H. E. Kimbal when I come away, and he agreed to see that you had clean clothes as often as necessary.

No one but God, knows the reflections of my mind and the feelings of my heart when I left our house and home, and almost all of everything that we possessed excepting our little Children, and took my journey out of the State of Missouri, leaving you shut up in that lonesome prison. But the reflection is more than human nature ought to bear, and if God does not record our sufferings and avenge our wrongs on them that are guilty, I shall be sadly mistaken.

The daily sufferings of our brethren in travelling, and camping out nights, and those on the other side of the river would beggar the most lively description. The people in this state are very kind indeed, they are doing much more than we ever anticipated they would; I have many more things I could like to write but have not time and you may be astonished at my bad writing and incoherent manner, but you will pardon all when you reflect how hard it would be for you to write, when your hands were stiffened with hard work, and your heart convulsed with intense anxiety. But I hope there is better days to come to us yet, Give my respects to all in that place that you respect, and am ever yours affectionately.

Joseph Smith Jr   Emma Smith

> The people in this state are very kind indeed, they are doing much more than we ever anticipated they would.[18]

Joseph Smith III later recalled his time on the Cleveland farm in his memoirs. Living nearby were the Huntingtons, another refugee family:

> Mother made no objection to our visiting the Huntington children until she learned by some means that Allen was in the habit of taking his father's gun out with him when we were over there. Being fearful some accident might happen by which some of us might lose our lives or be crippled, she bade us stay away from the Huntington house, explaining as she did so that she did not think Allen with his rifle a safe companion for little children.
>
> The game was fascinating, however, and I soon wandered over to the Huntington home again. Returning rather late, I was questioned by Mother, and had to admit that I had been out with the boys among the hazel brush, hunting for rabbits, and that Allen had carried the rifle. Thereupon, with the aid of a ready hazel switch, she promptly administered punishment.
>
> But the end was not yet. The next morning she said to Frederick and me—her command being upon me especially, since I was the older—"Joseph, I will not say you must not go to Mrs. Huntington's today, but I will say that if you do go I shall punish you when you return. It is a dangerous thing to play with Allen when he carries the rifle, and I am not going to be responsible for any harm that may come. So just remember what I tell you."
>
> Again, either forgetful or neglectful of the mandate, I ventured into the forbidden region and spent a portion of the day with the Huntington boys in the hazel brush after rabbits, staying late enough in the afternoon to see the little animals at play on the hillside and to hear the crack of the rifle.

Joseph Smith III later recalled his time on the Cleveland farm in his memoirs.

Liberty Jail
by C. C. A. Christensen

Joseph Jr. and other Church leaders continued to be held in Missouri jails until mid-April of 1839.

When I returned home Mother had company at supper and nothing was said to me about my visit to the Huntingtons; hence I went to bed thinking it had escaped my mother's notice and that I was safe from punishment. However, after the guests departed, I discovered my error, for Mother found me and I received the punishment she had promised, applied vigorously enough to make me feel sorry I had undressed as I went to bed!

When morning came Mother repeated her charge, saying, "I will not say you shall not go to play with the Huntington boys while their mother allows Allen to take his father's gun with him to play; but if you do go, I will punish you; and I shall punish you harder and harder until you stop."

Once more the allure of the pastime seemed stronger than my mother's counsel and her efforts to deter me, and again I went to the Huntington's and spent the day with the boys and their rifle. When I returned my mother punished me with such decidedly increased severity that I—well, comment is needless! I did not go again, for I found that my mother was indeed a woman of her word.[19]

Meanwhile, Joseph Jr. and other Church leaders continued to be held in Missouri jails until mid-April of 1839 when, while traveling to Columbia, Missouri, as part of a change of venue, they apparently bribed their guards, who then allowed them to escape.[20] Joseph and his fellow prisoners arrived safely in Quincy on April 22, 1839, and spent the next day greeting and being visited by their brethren and friends.[21] Regarding the escape of the prisoners, Lucy Mack Smith later wrote:

> When the news went abroad that the Smiths [Joseph and Hyrum] had been liberated and were now at home the Quincy Greys came down to our house and saluted them in the most polite manner our friends swarmed around us and we spent the day in eating and drinking and making merry.[22]

Joseph would spend two and a half weeks in and around Quincy. During that time, a general conference of the Church was held on May 4–6 at a Presbyterian campground just outside the city. Business of the conference included a decision to send Sidney Rigdon and other Church leaders to Washington, D.C., to begin petitioning the federal government to force Missouri to compensate Latter-day Saints for their losses in that state. Hundreds, if not thousands, of redress petitions were gathered and submitted. They survive to this day, documenting property lost as well as constitutional injuries suffered; a dollar value is assigned to each.[23] The conference also authorized John P. Greene to travel to New York City to oversee the congregation there and collect donations for the relief of the poor Saints gathering to Quincy.[24]

On May 4-6, 1839, a general conference of the Church at which Joseph Smith presided was held in Quincy. At that time, he was filled with great emotion to once again be with the Saints.

All of North and South America Is Zion
by George Lloyd

A May 6, 1839, introductory letter from Joseph Smith to John P. Greene reveals Joseph's concern for the poor in Quincy:

> And we beseech the Brethren [in New York] in the name of the Lord Jesus to receive this Brother [Greene] in behalf of the poor with readiness, and to abound unto him in a liberal manner, for "in as much as ye have done it unto the least of these, ye have done it unto me."
>
> Yours in the bonds of the everlasting gospel, though no longer a prisoner in the hands of the Missourians;
> And still faithful with the Saints
> Joseph Smith Jr Chairman.[25]

Also at the conference, a decision was made to sanction land purchases just upriver at the head of the Des Moines rapids on behalf of the Church. Known then as Commerce, this land would soon find fame under a new name: Nauvoo.

On May 9, 1839, Joseph Smith Jr. packed his family into a wagon and began the two-day trip to Nauvoo and the newly purchased Hugh White farm that included the two-story, two-room log house now known as the Homestead. Most Latter-day Saints in and around Quincy would soon follow to Nauvoo.[26]

Once settled in Nauvoo, Joseph didn't forget the kindness shown to him and others by the people of Quincy. On February 3, 1841, Joseph presented the following resolution to the Nauvoo City Council, which unanimously adopted it:

> Resolved by the City Council of the City of Nauvoo—that the Citizens of Quincy be held in everlasting remembrance for their unparalle[le]d liberality & marked kindness to our People, when in their greatest state of suffering & want.[27]

The charitable acts on behalf of the Latter-day Saints didn't end abruptly when the Saints left Quincy. The "Quincy Committee," comprised of leading citizens of the town, would negotiate a truce in the violent conflict during the fall of 1845 and arrange terms for the peaceful departure of the thousands of Latter-day Saints who followed Brigham Young west across the plains to the valley of the Great Salt Lake.[28] The committee intervened again in September of 1846 to end the Battle of Nauvoo, during which extralegal forces used cannons to drive remaining Church members from the city.[29] Emma Smith, by that time widowed as a result of the June 1844 assassination of Joseph and Hyrum Smith in Carthage, fled upriver to Fulton, Illinois, as the battle was breaking out.[30] She returned to Nauvoo with her children

Smith Homestead, Nauvoo, Illinois

Joseph Smith and his family moved into the Homestead in May 1839. At that time, only the right-hand, two-story log portion of the Homestead was standing.

five months later and lived out her life in Nauvoo, dying there in 1879.[31]

The people of Quincy invited the Smith family and the larger Church community in as strangers. They satisfied the Saints' hunger, quenched their thirst, provided them with clothing, and tended them in their sicknesses. Like the good Samaritan, they bandaged wounds, brought the homeless to the inn, and cared for those "in their greatest state of suffering & want." And for all of this, the good people of Quincy are remembered even today.

Lachlan Mackay

Lachlan Mackay serves as Director of Historic Sites for Community of Christ as well as Site Director of the Joseph Smith Historic Site. In these roles, he oversees properties in Ohio, Illinois, Iowa, and Missouri.

ENDNOTES

1. Joseph Smith, Sidney Rigdon, and Hyrum Smith, "A Proclamation of the First Presidency of the Church to the Saints Scattered Abroad," *Times and Seasons*, Jan. 15, 1841, 273–77.

2. Alexander L. Baugh, *A Call to Arms: The 1838 Mormon Defense of Northern Missouri* (Provo, UT: Joseph Fielding Smith Institute and BYU Studies, 2000), 149–54.

3. Richard P. Howard, ed., *The Memoirs of President Joseph Smith III (1832–1914)* (Independence, MO: Herald Publishing House, 1979), 4.

4. *Lucy's Book: A Critical Edition of Lucy Mack Smith's Family Memoir*, ed. Lavina Fielding Anderson (Salt Lake City: Signature Books, 2001), 681.

5. *Lucy's Book*, 681.

6. *Lucy's Book*, 682–83.

7. *Lucy's Book*, 684.

8. *Lucy's Book*, 684–85.

9. *Lucy's Book*, 686.

10. *Lucy's Book*, 686–87.

11. *Lucy's Book*, 687.

12. *Lucy's Book*, 692.

13. *Lucy's Book*, 693.

14. *Lucy's Book*, 693–94.

15. *Lucy's Book*, 695.

16. For a discussion of the 1839 population of Quincy and the number of Mormon refugees in and around Quincy, see Marlene C. Kettley, Arnold K. Garr, and Craig K. Manscill, "Quincy, Illinois: A Temporary Refuge, 1838–39, in *Mormon Thoroughfare: A History of the Church in Illinois, 1830–1839* (Provo, UT: Religious Studies Center, 2006), 91–112n6, 24.

17. Edward Partridge [Quincy, IL] to Joseph Smith and others [Liberty, MO], Mar. 5, 1839, in Joseph Smith Letterbook 2, 3–4; handwriting of James Mulholland. Joseph Smith Papers, Church History Library.

18. Emma Smith [Quincy, IL] to Joseph Smith [Liberty, MO], Mar. 7, 1839, in Joseph Smith Letterbook 2, 37; handwriting of James Mulholland. Joseph Smith Papers, Church History Library.

19. Howard, *Memoirs of President Joseph Smith III*, 5.

20. Howard, *Memoirs of President Joseph Smith III*, 6.

21. D. B. Huntington's statement of Joseph's landing on April 22, 1839, at Quincy, IL, as cited in Donna Hill, *Joseph Smith: The First Mormon* (Garden City, NY: Doubleday, 1977), 263.

22. *Lucy's Book*, 699.

23. Clark V. Johnson, ed., *Mormon Redress Petitions: Documents of the 1833–1838 Missouri Conflict* (Provo, Utah: Religious Studies Center, Brigham Young University, 1992)

24. Joseph Smith, History, 1838–1856, vol. C-1, Feb. 24, 1845–July 3, 1845, Church History Library; see also General Conference Minutes, May 4–6, 1839, Quincy, IL, Church History Library.

25. Joseph Smith, History, 1838–1856, vol. C-1; see also General Conference Minutes, May 4-6, 1839, Quincy, IL.

26. Joseph Smith, History, 1838–1856, vol. C-1; see also entries for May 9–10, 1839.

27. Joseph Smith, Resolution, Feb. 3, 1841, Nauvoo, IL, in Nauvoo City Council Minute Book, Feb. 3, 1841, 4–5; handwriting of James Sloan, Church History Library.

28. Marshall Hamilton, "From Assassination to Expulsion: Two Years of Distrust, Hostility, and Violence," in *Kingdom on the Mississippi Revisited: Nauvoo in Mormon History*, ed. Roger D. Launius and John E. Hallwas (Urbana and Chicago: University of Illinois Press, 1996), 223.

29. Hamilton, "From Assassination to Expulsion," 225.

30. Howard, *Memoirs of President Joseph Smith III*, 39.

31. Howard, *Memoirs of President Joseph Smith III*, 39, 186.

We of Quincy are proud of the badge of honor our community has been accorded as "A City of Refuge."

JOHN WOOD
and the Mormons

by Reg Ankrom

We of Quincy are proud of the badge of honor our community has been accorded as "A City of Refuge," reflected in the title of the wonderful book Susan Easton Black and Richard E. Bennett compiled at the beginning of the new millennium.[1] We hold our ancestors' spirit of humanity as the exemplar of the Golden Rule as they opened their hearts and homes to approximately 5,000 Mormons crossing the frozen Mississippi River in the winter of 1838–39 to escape annihilation. During that winter, this town of sixteen hundred residents provided shelter to an exhausted and destitute group of Latter-day Saints who had been ordered to leave Missouri or face extermination.[2]

Yet Quincy's welcome was not immediate. Newspapers circulating in town had affected local public opinion about the Mormons even before they began arriving. In September 1838, the *Quincy Daily Whig* voiced alarm about Mormons "threatening the lives of all known to be opposed to them."[3] The *Western Star* of Liberty, Missouri, reported that Mormons had been "committing outrages . . . (on) old and respectable citizens of Daviess County."

The *Daily Whig*, which carried the *Star* report, followed up by writing the shocking prediction that "from all appearances, there is trouble brewing. We should not be surprised, if the difficulty eventuated in much blood being shed."[4] Trouble followed Joseph Smith and other early Church members from the time E. B Grandin published the Book of Mormon in 1830. It followed them to Kirtland, Ohio, and to Far West, Missouri.

Little wonder, then, that as the destitute people of the struggling Mormon Church gathered across the river from Quincy that winter, waiting for ice to bridge the western and eastern shores, the residents of Quincy were apprehensive. Who were these people? Why would the governor of Missouri threaten them with extinction if they did not leave? Would violence follow them here?

Not only did the Saints' presence create anxiety in the city, it also created local controversy over who would extend relief to the Saints and why. The Democratic Association of Quincy took the lead in February 1839, and the *Quincy Whig* complained that the "contemptible object of this knot of third rate politicians" had no further aim than to gain Mormon affections—or, more likely, votes.[5] After all, many in this large group were white, male, twenty-one years of age or older, and soon-to-be residents of Illinois. Anyone meeting those four criteria under the state's ten-year-old constitution was eligible to vote. That large block of voters was attractive, and in a few years was the reason the new associate justice of the Illinois Supreme Court—Stephen A. Douglas, age twenty-seven—would insist that Governor Thomas Carlin appoint him to the judicial district headquartered in Quincy.

Douglas was an ambitious and impatient politician of the sort

> The citizens of Quincy are proud of their heritage of compassion and sacrifice.
>
> Quincy-Mississippi River Mormon marker #1
> 3 August 2002

Illinois had not seen before. Only four months earlier, he had engineered his appointment as secretary of state just to sign the charter that turned Commerce City, forty miles north of Quincy on the Mississippi, into the city of Nauvoo. That act—and the work Douglas performed to win the legislature's approval for it—had earned Douglas the affection of Joseph Smith. "Douglas is a Master Spirit," the Prophet proclaimed, "and his friends are our friends. . . . These men are free from prejudices and superstitions of the age, and such men we love, and such men will ever receive our support, be their political predilections what they may be."[6] Also a circuit judge, Douglas rejected from the bench Missouri appeals to return Smith and occasionally counseled his Mormon friends on matters of law. On occasion, Douglas was a guest in Smith's Nauvoo Mansion House.

Stephen A. Douglas, as secretary of state in Illinois, signed the charter for the new city of Nauvoo. The efforts of Douglas on behalf of the Latter-day Saints won him the affection and praise of the Prophet Joseph Smith.

With concerns about the Mormon mass of tattered humanity, a committee of Quincy's Democratic Association invited Sidney Rigdon, Joseph Smith's primary assistant, to explain the Mormons' plight. Rigdon had been incarcerated with brothers Joseph and Hyrum Smith at Liberty Jail in Missouri during their arrest in December 1838. Rigdon was released, however, when stricken ill. The Smiths were still there, awaiting trial for treason, as their Church followers huddled in the makeshift camp in and beyond Quincy's Washington Park, a half mile up the bluff from the Mississippi.

Whigs found out about the invitation to Rigdon and attended what was supposed to have been a closed meeting. Whig lawyer Nehemiah Bushnell criticized the Democrats for using what he called "pitiable intentions" for political gain and contended that assistance should be the work and gift of all citizens of Quincy.[7]

Rigdon's explanation was successful. Although it was the Democratic Association that reported Rigdon's statements, Bushnell's plea had had its effect. The association passed a series of resolutions determining that "the exiled strangers were entitled to the sympathy and aid of [all] the people of Quincy." The association called for a standing committee of members from every part of town to "allay the

When Nehemiah Bushnell, a Whig and an attorney, learned that the Quincy Democrats were meeting to determine how to help the Mormons, he contended that assistance should be the responsibility of all citizens of Quincy, not just Democrats.

prejudices of the misguided citizens of Quincy." It called for another standing committee "to relieve, so far as is in their power, the wants of the destitute and houseless, and . . . to use their utmost endeavors to procure employment for those who are able and willing to labor."

The committee added one more appeal: "We recommend to all citizens of Quincy that in all their intercourse with the strangers, they use and observe a becoming decorum and delicacy, and be particularly careful not to indulge in any conversation or expression calculated to wound their feelings, or in any way to reflect upon those who, by every law of humanity, are entitled to our sympathy and commiseration."[8]

The citizens of Quincy responded. Among them was John Wood, an easterner who in 1819 squatted and farmed in Pike County. In 1822, Wood bought his first 160 acres at the top of the bluff that would eventually become Quincy.

A great humanitarian effort like the one necessary to assist the Mormons would have suited Wood well. He had grown up at the eastern edge of the "Burned-Over District" in western New York. A great many religious gatherings were held there as part of the Second Great Awakening, a revivalist movement that drew thousands of converts in the early 1800s. Divorcing themselves from the severe doctrines of the Calvinists—that only by predestination could one enter the kingdom of heaven—innovative preachers taught worshippers that they could achieve their own salvation through good works. Reform movements followed, advocating abolition, temperance, universal education, aid to the suffering, and women's rights.[9] At this same time another religion was created in the "Burned-Over District," "delivered on tablets by an angel to young Joseph Smith."[10]

When John Wood left for the West in 1818, he brought with him this works-and-humanitarian spirit, and he put it to use almost as soon as he arrived in Illinois. Three years before the Missouri Territory entered the Union in 1821 as a slave state, Illinois entered the union. The men of Illinois's territorial legislature were Southerners, and they expected to shape their new state with Southern institutions. One of these was slavery. The number of slaves in Illinois in 1810 was 168. By 1820, two years after Illinois's admission to the Union, the number had grown to 917. The number of free Blacks over the decade had declined from 613 to 457.[11] The interest in slavery—and in ignoring its presence in Illinois—was clearly on the rise.

State legislators' intentions to enter the Union as a slave state had been thwarted by New York Congressman James Tallmadge Jr., who reminded the legislators that Illinois was part of the Northwest Territory, in which slavery was prohibited by Article 6 of the Northwest Ordinance. As a result, the legislature applied to enter the Union as a free state, reckoning that once in, they could amend their constitution to become a slave state. In such a maneuver, Congress

Leading the rally to help the Mormon refugees was John Wood, mayor and founder of Quincy.

John Wood, a native of western New York, grew to maturity on the eastern edge of the "Burned-Over District." He ventured west in 1818 and settled in Illinois.

Methodist Revival
Artist Unknown

Illinois became a state on December 3, 1818. The intention of leading politicians in Illinois, who had ties to the Southern states, was to amend the Illinois constitution to allow for slavery. John Wood worked to ensure that Illinois remained a free state.

Illinois Quarter Commemorating Illinois Statehood

had no authority to intervene. (The U.S. Constitution's only requirement for entry was that a state have a Republican form of government.)

Illinois became the Union's twenty-first state on December 3, 1818. In 1824, legislators placed on the ballot a referendum that, if successful, would seat a statewide convention to write slavery into the Illinois constitution. Appalled by the proposed move, John Wood helped organize and lead a crusade to defeat the proposal. He took on the responsibility of leading the opposition in the Military Tract, the five-million-acre wedge between the Illinois and Mississippi rivers. A number of young men, veterans of the War of 1812, had settled on bounty land they had received for their service. Wood made it his goal to ensure they voted against slavery.

The convention referendum was included in the August 23, 1824, election and lost statewide by a ratio of fifty-seven to forty-three.[12] In the Military Tract, where Wood led it, the ratio against slavery was ninety-six to four.[13] Of all he would accomplish in family, business, and government over his next

But what John Wood as a young man heard in New York right at the eastern edge of that so-called "Burned-Out District" of New York was that people had the ability to achieve their own salvation, and they could do it by good works. John Wood and his colleagues brought the idea of good works to western Illinois. And good works were moral works. That included temperance. It included women's suffrage in some areas, even as early as 1830 and 1840. It included the elimination of slavery, but it also included loving one's fellow human being and making sure that in good works, in good faith, that we do as Jesus told us: love our neighbor. And I think that was a part of the culture that came here that hadn't existed before. And in this very house in which we're seated, John and his wife took care of eighteen young girls whose families could not afford to keep them. He also took care of other people, including the Germans. John Wood provided land for four of the churches that still exist in Quincy. A very beneficent individual, he had from his heart a great feeling for human beings. —*Reg Ankrom*

fifty-eight years, Wood considered his part in the victory over slavery in Illinois his life's greatest achievement.[14]

Wood's friendship with Joseph Smith and the Mormons began with their arrival in Illinois and continued through their departure from the state. As mayor in 1843, Wood invited the Prophet and leaders of the Church to Quincy. Wood met Smith and his entourage at their boat, which had ferried them across the Mississippi. After giving his visitors a look at the town, Mayor Wood escorted them to his large Greek revival home on the northwest side of Wood and Burton Roads, about a mile up the bluff from the river. There they joined several other Quincy leaders and their wives for conversation and dinner. Afterward, "Brother Joseph" was said to have entertained so well that his hosts were "loath [sic] to have him depart."[15]

Professor Susan Easton Black noted that Joseph Smith wrote in his journal about his reciprocation: "Friday, July 14, 1843—I was visited by a number of gentlemen and ladies who had arrived from Quincy on a steamboat. They manifested kind feelings."

In July 1843, Joseph Smith and other Latter-day Saints dined at the John Wood Mansion. On that occasion, Joseph Smith remarked that his hosts were "loath [sic] to have him depart."

John Wood Mansion, The Historical Society of Quincy and Adams County

Battle of Nauvoo by C. C. A. Christensen

In late September 1846, anti-Mormon mobs attacked Nauvoo and drove the remaining Mormons out of the city. Citizens of Quincy attempted to negotiate a peaceful settlement to what became known as "The Battle of Nauvoo."

Another entry Black includes in her essay speaks to the intimacy of the friendship some residents of Quincy felt for their Mormon friends. Smith wrote in his journal, "Captain White, of Quincy, was at the Mansion last night, and this morning drank a toast saying, 'May Nauvoo become the empire seat of government!'"[16]

A little less than a year after that entry, Joseph and his brother Hyrum were dead, victims of a mob at the Hancock County Jail in Carthage on June 27, 1844. It was the beginning of the Mormon Wars and, ultimately, the departure of the Mormons from Illinois.

By the summer of 1846, many Saints had already left Illinois for "Deseret," or present-day Utah. Those who remained—generally the poorest, who were without the means to outfit themselves for the journey—were often intimidated and harassed.[17] And it was not just the Saints. Any in Nauvoo who were friendly to the Saints were threatened as well with the loss of life and property.[18]

At this point, William E. Clifford, president of the Nauvoo town board, appealed to Governor Thomas Ford for protection. Ford sent Major James R. Parker of the Illinois state militia, authorizing him to raise and command volunteers if Nauvoo was attacked. Anti-Mormon tempers rose as Parker recruited volunteers. A large mob rejected agreements their leaders had signed that exchanged quiet for a promise by the Mormons to leave Nauvoo within sixty days.

At mid-morning on September 10, watchmen in the tower of the Nauvoo Temple saw a horde estimated at seven hundred men approaching on Carthage Road. Major Parker ordered the four companies of volunteers he had recruited to march out to meet them.

At about the same time, Quincy mayor John Wood led a delegation of four other Quincy leaders into Nauvoo. It was said that they "were indignant at the villainous conduct of the mob towards an oppressed and defenseless community."[19] One of the delegation's members, Major William Flood, had been authorized by Governor Ford to raise forces in Adams County. Wood was anxious to avoid bloodshed, however, and proposed a meeting with the anti-Mormons to see if there was any chance to construct a compromise, which appeared to tilt the scales toward the insurrectionists with an aim to appease.

Under Wood's leadership, a series of concessions were reached:
- Writs against Mormons who had criminal charges filed against them would be served.
- Mormons would deliver up their weapons.
- Anti-Mormon forces would be able to enter the city, promising not to molest people or property unless attacked.

Wood may have left the anti-Mormon camp believing a peace had been achieved. Just how seriously his correspondents considered it, however, was demonstrated when, as the Quincy delegation left to return to Nauvoo, several cannon balls were fired over their heads.

There was no artillery in Nauvoo, but some enterprising residents retrieved two hollow steamboat shafts and made makeshift cannons, plugging the ends of the shafts with iron and test firing one of the cannons. Its thunder surprised the mob camp, sending a message that the town was better prepared than the mob had expected. With that, Mayor Wood and Joel Rice, a Quincy merchant, returned to the anti-Mormon camp to let their leaders know they would be attacking forces raised by Governor Ford's order. Wood's ploy failed. The mob told Mayor Wood they were resolved to drive the people from Nauvoo.

Following some strong skirmishing, mob leader Thomas Brockman sent a communication to Benjamin Clifford to surrender. Wood carried Clifford's answer to Brockman: Clifford would entertain any proposition that would avoid bloodshed.[20] The mob's response was to attack Nauvoo, and the first killings were recorded. The Nauvoo forces repulsed the mob on September 12.

Immediately after the battle, John Wood left for Quincy to give an account to the citizens of Quincy about what had happened in Nauvoo. Quincy leaders decided to form a committee of one hundred men to return with Wood to Nauvoo, believing they would be able to resolve the differences. When they arrived at Nauvoo, however, Wood and Rice were surprised to discover that many who had joined the Quincy committee were strongly anti-Mormon. Wood resigned membership in the committee and acted with a smaller group to negotiate with anti-Mormon leaders.

On September 16, as the mob resumed firing on Nauvoo, Wood's group of ten men negotiated another treaty with mob leaders. It called for

Quincy Historical Society

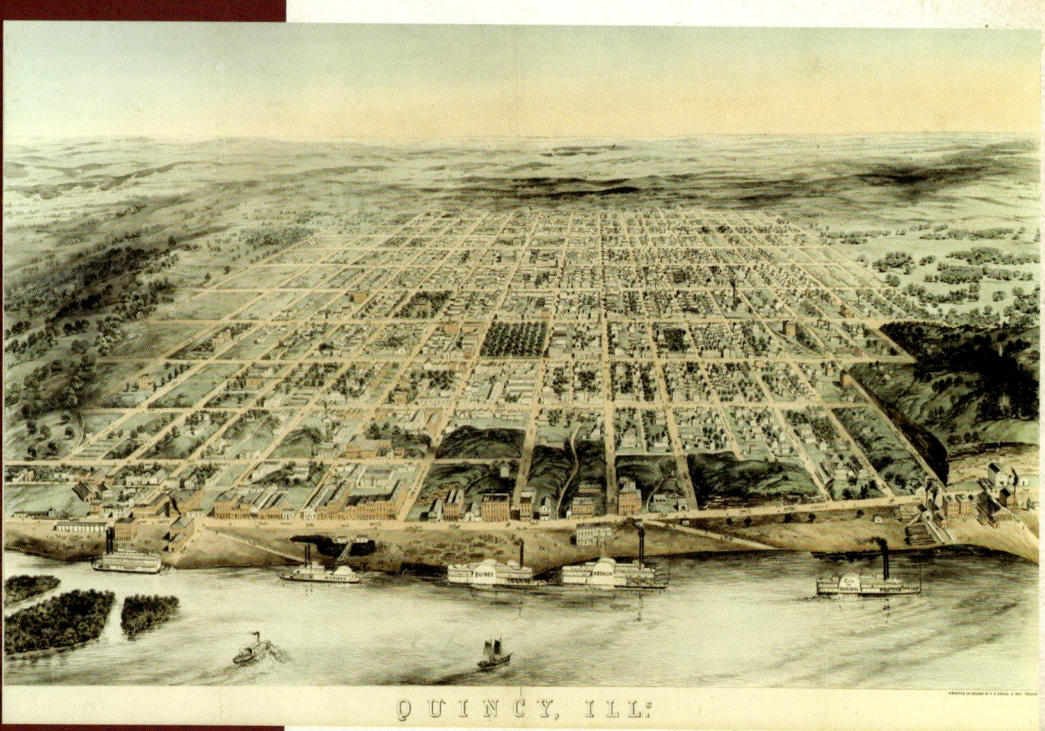

QUINCY, ILL.

Catching Quail
by C. C. A. Christensen

Anti-Mormon mobs drove the Saints across the Mississippi River. Mayor John Wood and other citizens of Quincy gathered food and supplies and ferried the products up river to assist the starving Saints.

- Hostilities to cease immediately.
- The Nauvoo force to surrender.
- Weapons to be delivered to the Quincy group.
- A promise from the Quincy group to use their influence to halt the violence in Nauvoo.
- Protection and care for the sick and helpless.
- The remaining Saints to depart as soon as they could cross the river.
- Five saints to remain in the city as trustees to dispose of property.
- Hostilities to cease immediately.

The Quincy ten were to return to Nauvoo to execute the provisions as they saw fit and proper.

The settlement irritated the remaining Mormons, but it was clear to Mormon esquire Daniel H. Wells that "there is no use in the small handful of volunteers trying to defend the city against such an overwhelming force.... Who could urge the propriety of exposing life to defend a place for the purpose of vacating it?"[21] Wells also feared that Wood's Quincy Committee was ready to join the mob if the treaty was not accepted. He recommended acceptance. When the treaty was in place, the state's militia volunteers disbanded.

On the morning of September 17, the non-Mormon force, said to number fifteen hundred, marched into the city and made the Nauvoo Temple their headquarters. Ignoring the promises of the treaty their leaders had just made, the force entered houses, plundered Mormon holdings, and threatened families. At the river, they searched wagons belonging to the Saints waiting to cross and confiscated arms and ammunition. The Saints' condition was desperate. The *St. Louis Reveille* reported that the Saints "crossed the river and made an encampment on the banks of the Mississippi, opposite Nauvoo." The people there, said the newspaper, were "starving under the open heavens with not even a tent to cover them."[22] From the west side of the Mississippi in Montrose, Iowa, the Saints could look back to see the tower of their temple. It was here that John Wood performed his final humanitarian service before these last of the Latter-day Saints began their journey west.

John Wood was responsible for the assistance that citizens of Quincy provided as the Mormons departed from Illinois into Iowa. He knew they were destitute. They had very little. It was almost the same condition as when they arrived and the Quincy people assisted with food and shelter and clothing then. 00:40:11 What he saw at that time was the tremendous need for clothing, tremendous need for food, and they did need money. And when John Wood returned to Quincy from Nauvoo in late September of 1846, he and Henry Asbury and Mr. Cairns and others suggested to their neighbors that we provide food and clothing and provide whatever money we can afford to those who were now going across the river. And it was very few at that point. Most of them had gone across. But a steamboat was loaded with whatever materials people provided. And it was taken up the river and those materials and money were delivered to the Mormons in Montrose the following day. —*Reg Ankrom*

Organization of the Relief Society by Robert T. Barrett

In 1842, when the Female Relief Society of Nauvoo was organized and Emma Smith was called as its first president, she selected Sarah Cleveland, the woman who sheltered her in Quincy, to be her counselor. The gratitude expressed by Emma on that occasion carries to the present day. Latter-day Saints continue to express gratitude for the citizens of Quincy and their kindness so long ago.

Wood and William Karnes, a co-owner of the *Quincy Argus* newspaper, crossed the river to visit the Mormons' Montrose encampment. Wood and Karnes found the Saints "in need of all kinds of clothing, materials for tents, shoes, &c."[23]

Lawyer Henry Asbury recalled that when he returned to Quincy, "[Wood] represented to us that they [the Mormons] were in a very destitute condition. Our committee resolved that upon returning home we should at once set about collecting money, clothing and provisions to be forwarded to these people. . . . We carried out this resolution by collecting a large sum of money and provisions and clothing, which was sent to them."[24] In a broadside quickly circulated throughout Quincy, Wood indicated the urgency of the need by suggesting that contributions be sent to the Saints on the next steamboat to leave Quincy.[25]

Conclusion

The Prophet Joseph Smith had arrived in Quincy on April 22, 1839, where he had reunited with his wife Emma and their four children at the home of John and

Sarah Cleveland. John Cleveland had helped Wood design and build the large Greek revival mansion in Quincy, which Smith and other Nauvoo officials and their wives would visit. Sarah Cleveland, already a Mormon, would become first counselor to Emma Smith at the creation of the women's Relief Society in 1842.

Joseph Smith expressed his gratitude to the Mississippi River community whose residents had helped the Saints in their time of need. Among those, the Prophet said, who deserved special mention, "whose kindness, on that occasion, is indelibly engraved on the tablets of our hearts in golden letters of love," was John Wood, who attended them from the time of their arrival to their departure.[26]

Reg Ankrom

Reg Ankrom is the author of *Stephen A. Douglas: The Political Apprenticeship, 1833–1843*. The first of three books he is writing about Douglas, this first includes a detailed examination of the relationship of Douglas and Mormon Prophet Joseph Smith, as well as the role of the City of Quincy in providing refuge to Latter Day Saints expelled from Missouri during the winter of 1838-39. Ankrom earned a bachelor's degree from Illinois College in Jacksonville and his master's from the University of Kansas. He and wife Jane live in Quincy.

ENDNOTES

1. *Quincy: A City of Refuge*, ed. Susan Easton Black and Richard E. Bennett (Salt Lake City: Millennial Press, 2000).

2. "Missouri Executive Order 44," issued by Governor Lilburn W. Boggs, Oct. 27, 1838.

3. "The Mormons," *Quincy Daily Whig*, Sept. 8, 1838, 3.

4. "The Mormons," 3.

5. Iris Nelson, "Once upon a Time in Quincy: Arrival of the Destitute Mormons in 1839," *Quincy Herald-Whig*, Mar. 9, 2014.

6. Reg Ankrom, *Stephen A. Douglas: The Political Apprenticeship, 1833–1843* (Jefferson, NC: McFarland & Co., 2015), 356; Joseph Smith, "State Gubernatorial Convention," *Times and Seasons*, Dec. 20, 1841, 651; Manuscript History of the Church, vol. C-1, 436.

7. Nelson, "Once upon a Time in Quincy."

8. *Historical Record*, ed. Andrew Jensen (Salt Lake City: Andrew Jensen, 1888), 734.

9. Nathan Hatch, *The Democratization of American Christianity* (New Haven, CT: Yale University Press, 1989), 64.

10. Charles M. Wiltse, *The New Nation, 1800–1845* (New York: Hill and Wang, 1961), 136.

11. Jos. C. G. Kennedy, *Preliminary Report on the Eighth Census, 1860* (Washington, D.C.: Government Printing Office, 1862), 126–27.

12. Theodore Calvin Pease, *Illinois Election Returns, 1818–1848* (Springfield, IL: Illinois State Historical Library, 1923).

13. Reg Ankrom, "John Wood Fights Slavery in Illinois," *Quincy Herald Whig*, Aug. 26, 2012.

14. Reg Ankrom, "The True John Wood," presentation to POLIS, Quincy University, Sept. 16, 2014.

15. *Quincy: City of Refuge*, 89–90.

16. *Quincy: City of Refuge*, 90.

17. *Historical Record*, 845.

18. The story of this period is found in "Battle of Nauvoo," *Historical Record*, 845–57.

19. "Chapters from the History of the Church," *Millennial Star*, Jan. 7, 1873, 10.

20. "Chapters from the History of the Church," 853.

21. *Historical Record*, 855.

22. A. William Lund, "Stories of the Pioneer Trail," *Improvement Era*, July 1928, 733.

23. Cecil K. Byrd, *A Bibliography of Illinois Imprints, 1814–58*. (Chicago: University of Chicago Press, 1966), 226.

24. Asbury, *Reminiscences of Quincy*, 168.

25. Byrd, *Bibliography of Illinois Imprints*, 226.

26. *Quincy: City of Refuge*, 94n.

Eliza R Snow
by Julie Rogers

Out of a heart full of gratitude and understanding, Zion's Poetess Eliza R. Snow composed the following poetic tribute to the citizens of Quincy.

TO THE
CITIZENS of QUINCY

Eliza R. Snow

Ye Sons and Daughters of Benevolence,
Whose hearts are tun'd to notes of sympathy
Who have put forth your liberal hand to meet
The urgent wants of the oppress'd and poor!

      Ye high-ton'd spirits; who have nobly dar'd
To stem the foaming tide of vile reproach,
And brave the pois'nous, deadly current of
Detraction and fell hate; in rescuing
Oppressed innocence, from the hard hand
Of the Oppressor!

          In return for this,
Though it perpetuates your City's name
And makes the sound of Quincy, echo sweet
And full of moral meaning to the soul
Of ev'ry true philanthropist: you get
No regal honors.—No loud trump of fame
Will blazon forth your deeds, except to throw
A dark'ning shade upon them; thus to aim
A cruel missile at the rescued ones.

No laurel branch nor cypress bough will wave
In graceful dignity about your heads, to tell,
In speechless eloquence what you have done.
No sculptur'd marble monument, will rear
Its head, as if in bold defiance to
The stern, untiring, withering hand of Time,
To teach your name and deeds to passers-by.
 No; we have no insignia of this kind—
No medal of an earthly mould to give:
But yet, we fain would proffer you a boon
Of more congenial texture—one that's wrought
In the fine fibres of the human heart,
Not in that heart where selfishness, and mean,
And low, and sordid feelings sit enthron'd:
And whose dull pulses are like clods confin'd
By the unwieldy chains of Ignorance.
For there are some, who, "privily have crept
Among us unawares" whose hearts are set
On gain, for filthy lucre's sake:—and while
We say to you, BEWARE OF SUCH, lest they
Abuse your liberality—we say,
Esteem them our MISFORTUNE, not our FAULT;
For tares must grow among the wheat, until
The time of harvest; therefore, the upright,

Must often suffer an unjust reproach.
   Pure Gratitude, our free-will off'ring, is
The product of an elevated mind;
When the heart beats with sensibility—
Reciprocates each high-born thought, and stoops
Unask'd, to pay its def'rence at the shrine—
The sacred shrine of generosity.
And SOME, yes, MANY, spirits such as these,
We have among us;—Noble minded ones,
Who will not swerve from those unchanging laws—
The steadfast principles of righteousness:—
Whose firm integrity would yet remain
Unmov'd tho' "mountains skip like rams, and all
The little hills like lambs."
                        The Gratitude
Which emanates from spirits such as these;
Is no mean offering-neither cheaply won—
Ye noble, gen'rous hearted Citizens
Of Quincy!

Eliza R. Snow, "To the Citizens of Quincy," *Poems Religious, Historical, and Political* 2 vols. (Liverpool: Latter-day Saints' Book Depot, 1856): 63-65; *Quincy Whig*, 11 May 1839

"Ye noble, gen'rous hearted Citizens Of Quincy!"
—Eliza R. Snow

Hopeful Deliverance, by Julie Rogers

Grateful for the Kindness

"Great God! have I not seen it? Yes, my eyes have beheld the blood-stained traces of innocent women and children, in the drear winter who had traveled hundreds of miles barefoot, through frost and snow, to seek a refuge from their savage pursuers."

—*Orville H. Browning*

Who were these people that attorney Orville H. Browning spoke about? They were approximately 5,500 Latter-day Saints fleeing from an extermination order in the state of Missouri to the barge town of Quincy. The following list—compiled by searching journals, autobiographies, LDS records, periodicals, and genealogical databases—is representative of the thousands who received welcomed assistance from the citizens of Quincy in the winter of 1839.

A

Ammon Abbott
Eliza Ann Abbott
Lewis Abbott
Rufus Abbott
Azra Adams
David W. Adams
Phebe Adams
Elijah Abel
Elizabeth Alden
William Aldrich
James H. Aldridge
Sophia Aldridge
William Aldridge
Horace M. Alexander
John Quincy Adams Alexander
Myra Alexander
Nancy Ann Naomi Alexander
Randolph Alexander
Susan Arabella Alexander
Thomas Murphy Alexander
John Alleman
Abram Allen
Alanson David Allen
Albern Allen
Almira Gilbert Allen
Anna Allen
Caroline Allen
Caroline Matilda Allen
Charles William Allen
Daniel Allen
Elihu Marcellus Allen
Elihu Moroni Allen
Elijah Allen
Gideon Allen
Joseph S. Allen
Lucinda Allen
Lucy Gunn Allen
Marcia Allen
Mary Ann Allen
Mary Elizabeth Allen
Nelson Allen
Rufus Allen
Andrew F. Allred
Andrew Jackson Allred
Barton B. Allred
David H. Allred
Eliza Maria Allred
Green W. Allred
Hannah Caroline Allred
Isaac Allred
Isaac N. Allred
James Allred
Martin C. Allred
Orissa A. Allred
R. A. Allred
Reddick Newton Allred
Reuben W. Allred
William Allred
William Moore Allred
Charlotte Alvord
Joseph B. Alvord
Thaddeus Alvord
Clarissa Ames
Ira Ames
Buckley Anderson
John Anderson
Lydia Anderson
Mary Anderson
Rachel Mahala Anderson
Abigail Andrews
Benjamin Andrews
James Andrus
Mary Jane Andrus
Milo Andrus
Almira Angel
Caroline Frances Angel
Emily Angel
Martha Ann Angel
Phebe Angel
Polly Ann Angel
Solomon Angel
Truman O. Angel
John C. Annis
John Archer
Margaret Ault
Richard Ault
Ann Austin
Emily Austin
Joseph B. Austin
Mary Austin
Elijah Averett
Elisha Averett
George Washington Averett
John Averett
William Averett
Arvin Avery
Daniel Avery
Philander Avery

B

Adolphus Babcock
Eliza Babcock
George Babcock
Lorenzo Babcock
Lucy Babcock
Permelia Babcock
Sophronia Babcock
John Badger
Lucy Badger
Rodney Badger
Alexander Badham
Cynthia Baggs
Eli Bagley
Jesse Baker
Sally Baker
Asher Baldwin
Caleb C. Baldwin
Nathan B. Baldwin
Helen Ballantyne
Barbara Eleanor Ballard
Elizabeth Shumate Ballard
Philip Ballard
Sarah Ann Ballard
William B. Ballard
Almira Barber
Eliza Haven Barlow
Israel Barlow
Jonathan W. Barlow
Richard Barlow
Lucinda Barlow
Watson Barlow
Eliza Ann W. Barnard
Ezra Jacob W. Barnard
John Porter Barnard
John Porter Barnard Jr.
Mary Louisa Barnard
Mormon Lachoneus Barnard
Ransom Barnard
Amanda Barnes
Asa W. Barnes
D. H. Barnes
Ezekiel Barnes

Huldah Barnes
Samuel Barnett
Edson Barney
Charles Barnum
Ethan Barrows
Archibald Bates
Sarah Marinda Bates
William Batson
Jonathan Beckelshymer
Henry Beckstead
Calvin Beebe
Eliza Ann Beebe
Isaac Beebe
Lucina Beebe
Isaac Behunin
Louisa Beman
Mary Adeline Beman
Christiana Benner
Henry Benner
David Bennett
Alva Benson
Benjamin Benson
Cynthia Vail Benson
David Benson
Jerome M. Benson
Polly Averia Benson
Richard Benson
Mary Kilburn Bent
Samuel Bent
Harriet Benton
Jacinth Bernell
Henry Best
Elizabeth Beswick
Henry H. Bett
Jane Adaline Bickmore
Elizabeth Roe Bidwell
Joseph Bidwell
Robert William Bidwell
Bathsheba Bigler
Henry W. Bigler
Jacob G. Bigler
Alfred Nelson Billings
Diantha Morley Billings
George Pierce Billings
Titus Billings

Titus Billings Jr.
Erastus Bingham
James R. Bingham
Sanford Bingham
Thomas Bingham
Benjamin F. Bird
Bradford Kennedy Bird
Charles Bird
Mary Ann Kennedy Bird
Phineas R. Bird
Zebiah Birdeno
Anna Marie Bishop
Abner Blackburn
Sarah Blackman
Stephen Blackman
Aseph Blanchard
P. Blanchard
Joseph Blodget
Newman Blodget
Roswell Blood
William Bolton
Edmund Bosley
William Bull Bosley
Mary Ann Bosworth
Daniel Bowen
Benjamin Boyce
Peter Boyce
Abraham Dodge Boynton
Eliphalet Boynton
Olive Boynton
Squire Bozarth
Truman Brace
James Bennett Bracken
Levi Bracken
James Braden
Elizabeth Hendrickson Brady
Lindsay Anderson Brady
Marion Hendrickson Brady
Benjamin Bragg
Phebe Bray
Richard Brazier
Ziphronia W. Brewster

Alexander Brim
Andrew Brim
Phebe Brook
George Washington Brooks
Lester Brooks
Alanson Brown
Alexander Brown
Albert Brown
Alfred Brown
Benjamin Brown
Cornelia Brown
Ebenezer Brown
Emily Sophia Brown
Francis Brown
Lorenzo Brown
Lydia Maria Lathrop Brown
Samuel Brown
Samuel Webster Brown
Sherman G. Brown
John Brownell
Harriet Gould Brunson
Lewis Brunson
Seymour Brunson
Elizabeth Buchanan
John Buchanan
Peter Buchanan
George W. Buell
John Hyrum Buell
Norman Buell
Oliver Normal Buell
Precinda Huntington Buell
Jane Draper Bulkley
Newman Bulkley
Alden Burdick
Catherine Burdick
Charlotte Burdick
Columbus B. Burdick
Eveline Burdick
Jerusha Cecilia Burdick
Jerusha Parks Burdick
Laura Louisa Burdick
Lubellus Burdick

Lucy Burdick
Marinda Burdick
Thomas Burdick
Elizabeth Burgess
Horace Burgess
Mariah Pulsipher Burgess
Vilate Burgess
William Burgess Jr.
William Burgess Sr.
Abi S. Burk
Charles Allen Burk
John Matthias Burk
Phoebe Jane Burk
Elizabeth Ann Burkett
George Burkett
William Burkett
Andrew Burnham
Emily Frances Burnham
Harriet Kimball Burnham
James Burnham
Enoch Burns
Abigail Burr
Horace Burr
William Burton
Caroline Elizabeth Butler
Caroline Skeen Butler
Charity Butler
Charles Butler
John Lowe Butler
Julia Ann Butler
Kenion T. Butler
Keziah Jane Butler
Lovisa Butler
Lucy Ann Butler
Ormond Butler
Phoebe Malinda Butler
Sarah Butler
Thomas S. Butler
Abel Butterfield
Benjamin Butterfield
Jacob K. Butterfield
Josiah Butterfield
Louisa Butterfield

Mary Jane Butterfield
Thomas Butterfield
David Byer
Hiram Byington

C

Arthur Cady
Amos Reynolds Cahoon
Andrew Cahoon
Daniel Stiles Cahoon
Lerona Eliza Cahoon
Louisa Cahoon
Mahonri Moriancumer Cahoon
Nancy M. Cahoon
Pulaski S. Cahoon
Reynolds Cahoon
Thirza S. Cahoon
William F. Cahoon
Abigail Calkins
Chauncey Calkins
Edwin Calkins
Hannah Calkins
Lemira Calkins
Lucy Calkins
Anson Call
Anson V. Call
Cyril Call
Fanny Call
Harvey Call
Homer Call
Josiah Call
Lucina Call
Mary F. Call
Melissa Call
Omer Call
Robert Campbell
S. Rosaline Call
Samantha Call
Sarah Call
Sarah Campbell
Caroline Card
Cyrus W. Card
David M. Card
William F. Card

William Carey
Daniel Carn
John B. Carpenter
Joseph S. Carrelton
Thomas Carrico
James Carroll
Rhoda Carroll
George Carson
John Carson
William Carson
Charles Carter
Clarissa Carter
Daniel Carter
Dominicus Carter
Jabez Carter
Joanna Carter
John Carter
John H. Carter
Lucinda Carter
Margaret Carter
Marietta Carter
Orlando Henry Carter
Phebe W. Carter
Simeon Doget Carter
Thomas Carter
William Carter
William F. Carter
Nancy Cary
Francis C. Case
Sarah Ann Casper
Thomas D. Casper
William W. Casper
Daniel Cathcart
Lorenzo D. Chamberlain
Polly Chamberlain
Solomon Chamberlain
Amanda Chapman
Amelia Chapman
Huldah Chapman
Isaac B. Chapman
Isaac Moroni Chapman
Jacob K.Chapman
Jane Chapman
Joseph Smith Chapman
Julia Chapman

Rosetta Annie Chapman
Susan A. Chapman
Welcome Chapman
Darwin J. Chase
Eli Chase
Hiram B. Chase
Isaac Chase
Stephen Chase
Amasa F. Cheney
Elam Cheney
Elijah Cheney
Elisa Ann Cheney
Eliza Jane Cheney
Ephraim Cheney
Helen Marr Cheney
Nathan Calhoun Cheney
Olive M. Cheney
Oren Cheney
Zacheus Cheney
William Cherry
Eunice Chidester
Jared Chidester
John M. Chidester
John Peck Chidester
Mary P. Chidester
Alfred B. Childs
Hannah P. Childs
John L. Childs
Lydia Ann Childs
Myron B. Childs
Nathaniel Childs
Orville R. Childs
Phoebe W. Childs
Polly Ann Childs
Warren G. Childs
Amanda W. Chipman
James Chipman
Stephen Chipman
Washburn Chipman
William H. Chipman
Eliza Jane Churchill
Lucina Churchill
Benjamin L. Clapp
Frank L. Clapp

Joseph C. Clapp
Mary S. Clapp
Molly E. Clapp
William Clapp
Catherine Clapper
J. Christian Clapper
Jacob Clapper
Mary Clapper
Caroline Clark
Enoch Clark
Ezra T. Clark
Harriet Clark
Hiram Clark
Isaac Clark
James A. Clark
John Wesley Clark
Joseph Clark
Joseph C. Clark
Lorenzo Clark
Maria B. Clark
Orphy Clark
Rodman Clark
Silas B. Clark
Timothy B. Clark
William O. Clark
Cornelia Clawson
Lola Ann Clawson
Moses Clawson
Wallace Clawson
Ada W. Clements
Albert Clements
Alvin Clements
Eliza Clements
Elizabeth Clements
James Clements
Lucy Clements
Paul Clements
John Cleminson
Lydia Cleminson
Adelia M. Clemons
Ann S. Cleveland
George W. Cleveland
Henry A. Cleveland
Henry Rogers Cleveland
Isaac Cleveland

Lydia Clisbee
Lyman Clisby
Ira Clothier
Benjamin Cluff
David Cluff Jr.
David Cluff Sr.
Elizabeth H. Cluff
Harvey Cluff
Joseph Cluff
Lavina Cluff
Moses M. Cluff
Samuel Cluff
William W. Cluff
Almon D. Clyde
Cynthia D. Clyde
Edward P. Clyde
George Washington Clyde
James Heber Clyde
Lucy Clyde
Solomon D. Clyde
William M. Clyde
Alanson Colby
Barnett Cole
Lucinda E. Cole
Nancy P. Cole
Nathan Owen Cole
Nelson Owen Cole
Owen Cole
Phebe A. Cole
William R. Cole
James Collins
Graham Coltrin
Henry C. Coltrin
John Coltrin
Sarah M. Coltrin
Zebedee Coltrin
Anthony Combs
Simeon J. Comfort
Ahaz Cook
Agnes M. Coolbrith
Joseph Wellington Coolidge
Libbeus Coons
Lucy Corkins

John Corrill
Almira Covey
Benjamin Covey
Enoch Covey
Joseph Covey
Eliza Ann Cowan
Horace Cowan
Robert Cowan
Austin Cowles
Elvira Annie Cowles
Amelia Cox
Amos Cox
Charles Thomas Cox
Emeline Cox
Frederick W. Cox Jr.
Frederick W. Cox Sr.
Louisa Jane Cox

Philena Cox
Ralph Cox
Benjamin Crandall
Daniel M. Crandall
Jacob Crandall
John W. Crandall
Luman Crandall
Myron N. Crandall
Patrick Crandall
Thomas Crandall
Sally Crandle
Simeon Crandle
Sarah W. Crane
David Crenshaw
Absalom Crichfield
Charles Crimson
Jonathan Crosby
Munro Crosier
George W. Crouse
Andrew Cunningham
Amanda Ann Curtis
Charlotte Curtis
David Avery Curtis
Emeline B. Curtis
Enos Curtis
Ezra Houghton Curtis
Jeremiah Curtis

Jacob Curtis
Joseph Curtis
Julia Curtis
Lyman Curtis
Martha Jane Curtis
Mary Curtis
Mecham Curtis
Moses Curtis
Nahum Curtis
Percy Curtis
Simons P. Curtis
Uriah Curtis
Alpheus Cutler
Benjamin F. Cutler
Clarissa Cutler
Louisa E. Cutler
Thaddeus Cutler

D

Almira B. Daley
Enoch R. Daley
James Daley
John Daley
Mary Matilda Daley
Moses Daley Jr.
Moses Daley Sr.
Phineas Daley
Cyrus Daniels
James E. Daniels Jr.
Lehi Daniels
Reuben Daniels
Sheffield Daniels
Solomon Daniels
Pamelia Darrow
George Davidson
Joseph S. Davidson
Abigail Davis
Alpha C. Davis
Anne Davis
Arza Davis
Cynthia Davis
Eleanor Jane Davis
James Spencer Davis
Jared Moroni Davis
Joseph M. Davis

Lysander Davis
Sarah Bell Davis
Sarah M. Davis
Sarah R. Davis
William Davis
Ann Dayton
Hiram Dayton
Maria Dayton
Moroni Dayton
Moses M. Dayton
Permelia Dayton
Permelia M. Dayton
Wallace W. Dayton
Henry Deam
Harriet Amelia Decker
Isaac Decker
Jacob DeGraw
Sophia DeGraw
David C. Deming
Adelia DeMille
Anna K. DeMille
Elias DeMille
Freeman DeMille
Laura Ann DeMille
Maria DeMille
Mariah DeMille
Oliver DeMille
David C. Deming
Jefferson Dimmick
Solomon W. Denton
Eliza Ann Dibble
Emma C. Dibble
Philander Dibble
Philo Dibble
Sidney Dibble
David Dille
Harriett Dille
Rachel Dilworth
David Dixon
Joseph Dobson
Augustus Erastus Dodge
Enoch E. Dodge
Erastus Dodge
Melissa Morgan Dodge

Seth George Dodge
Zenos W. Dodge
Eliza Dollinger
Thomas Dollinger
Charles Dolton
Mary E. Dolton
Peter Dopp
David D. Dort
Calvin C. Downey
Harvey Downey
Sarah Downing
Amy Emily Downs
Daniel Newel Drake
Alfred Draper
Lydia Draper
Polly Draper
Ruth Draper
Thomas Draper
William Draper Jr.
William Draper Sr.
Zemira Draper
Ellen Driggs
Hannah Driggs
Lorenzo Driggs
Shadrack Driggs
Urial Driggs
Rachel Drollinger
Charles H. Drury
Joel Drury
Pamelia H. Drury
Ruth Drury
Hannah Ann Dubois
James Dudley
Joseph Dudley
Moses Dudley
William Dudley
Chapman Duncan
Homer Duncan
John Duncan
Elizabeth Dunn
James Dunn
Eunice Dunning
Edmund Durfee
Elisabeth Durfee
Jabez Durfee

James Durfee
John Durfee
Julia Ann Durfee
Moroni Durfee
Nephi Durfee
Perry Durfee
Thomas Durfee
Edmund Durphy Jr.
Ether Durphy
Francillo Durfey
Bechias Dustin
Cyrena E. Dustin
David K. Dustin
Peter Dustin
Jane Dutcher
Ann Dutson
David Dutton
Edward P. Duzette
Rachel Dwelinger
George P. Dykes

E

Lewis Eager
Elias Eames
Ruggles Eames
Asa C. Earl
James E. Earl
Sylvester H. Earl
William Earl
William J. Earl
David Eds
Edward E. Edwards
Elisha F. Edwards
Esia Edwards
Harrison M. Edwards
James R. Edwards
Rufus Edwards
Elvira Egbert
John Egbert
Joseph T. Egbert
Robert C. Egbert
Samuel Egbert
Bradford W. Elliott
David Elliott
Roxey L. Elliott

Harriet Hales Ellis
John Ellis
Mary Ann Ellis
Josiah Ells
Josiah Elmer
James Emmet Jr.
James Emmet Sr.
Phebe Emmet
Charles English
Lydia B. English
Sarah B. Esterbrook
Christina Ettleman
Clara Ann Ettleman
Henry Ettleman
Jacob Ettleman
Phillip Ettleman
David Evans
Israel Evans
Susan Evertson
Francis M. Ewell
John P. Ewell
Pleasant Ewell
William F. Ewell

F

Joshua Fairchild
Susan Fairchild
Aaron F. Farr
Lorin Farr
Winslow Farr
John M. Fausett
William McGee Fausett
John Felshaw
William Felshaw
Isaac Ferguson
Warren Haskell Ferguson
Mercy Rachel Fielding
Edmond Fisher
Evelina Fisher
Joseph Fisher
Mary Ann Fisher
Polly Fisher
Thomas J. Fisher
Alfred Fisk

Hezekiah Fisk
Louisa Follett
Isaac Follis
Almira Foote
David Foote
Reuben R. Foote
Stephen V. Foote
Timothy B. Foote
Warren Foote
Rufus Forbush
Jonathan Ford
Mary Ford
Moroni Ford
William Ford Jr.
Elijah Fordham
George Fordham
Clarissa Fordish
Oliver Forester
Frederick Forney
John Forney
Mary Ann Forney
Clarissa Fosdick
John Fossett
William M. Fossett
Charles A. Foster
Clarissa A. Foster
James Foster
Julia Foster
Solon Foster
Sophia Foster
Catherine Foutz
Elizabeth Foutz
Jacob Foutz
Joseph Lehi Foutz
Margaret Foutz
Margaret M. Foutz
Susan Foutz
Nancy Fowler
Samuel Fowler
David Frampton
Nathaniel Frampton
Sarah Frampton
Abiah Franklin
Absalom Free
Andrew Free

Betsy S. Free
Finley C. Free
Hannah C. Free
Louisa Free
Mary Amanda Free
Preston Free
Telitha Free
Isaac F. Freeman
Solomon Freeman
Mary Ann Frost
William A. Fry
Amos B. Fuller
Catharine Fuller
Isaac Fuller
Luther Fuller
Samuel Fuller
David Fullmer
Desdemona W. Fullmer
Eugene B. Fullmer
Hannibal O. Fullmer
John S. Fullmer
Rhoda Ann Fullmer
Daniel Buckley Funk
Sarah Ann Funk

G

Elizabeth Gallaher
William C. Gallaher
David Gamet
Daniel Garn
David Garn
Emma Garn
Eveline Garn
Margaret Garn
Mary Ann Garn
Samuel Garn
David Garner Jr.
Jacob Gates
Thomas Gates Sr.
Eunice B. Gaylord
Joanna Gaylord
John Gaylord
Lester Gaylord
Amanda S. Gee
Elias Smith Gee

George W. Gee
Lysander Gee
Mary Jane Gee
Orlando Lysander Gee
Mary Gibbs
Sarah Gibbs
Alpheus Gifford
Levi Gifford
Levi Gifford Jr.
Moses Gifford
Samuel K. Gifford
Mary H. Gilbert
Sherman A. Gilbert
Fidilia Gillett
Truman Gillett
Flora Gleason
Elisha G. Goff
James Goff
John H. Goff
Martha Ellen Goff
Mary Goff
Sarah Jane Goff
Persis Goodall
Thomas C. Gordon
John Gould
William Gould
Carlos Granger
Oliver Granger
Sarah Granger
George Davis Grant
Jedediah Morgan Grant
Joshua Grant
George Graybill
Joseph Levi Graybill
Levi Graybill
Mary Graybill
Patience Graybill
William A. Graybill
Betsy Green
Harvey Green
Rosilla Green
Silas Green
Tanner C. Green
William Green
Addison Greene

Amanda Hoyt Greene
Evan M. Greene
Fanny E. Greene
Henrietta Green
John P. Greene
Nancy Z. Greene
Selah Griffin
Alameda Griffith
Judah Griffith
Michael Griffith
Adaline Grover
Caroline W. Grover
Emeline Grover
Thomas Grover
Elisha H. Groves
Elisha Samuel Groves
John S. Groves
Mary Groves
James Guyman
Noah T. Guyman

H

Reuben Hadlock
Stephen Hadlock
Alma Helaman Hale
Aroet Hale
Jonathan Harriman Hale
Olive B. Hale
Rachel Hale
Solomon Henry Hale
Charles Henry Hales
Eliza Anna Hales
Julia Ann Hales
Mary Isabella Hales
Benjamin K. Hall
Catharine Hall
Charles Hall
Elizabeth Hall
Horace L. Hall
Clark Hallett
Louisa Hallett
Phebe Hallett
Thatcher Clark Hallet
James B. Hamilton
John Hammond

Joseph Hammond
Mary A. Hammond
Sophronia Hammond
John Hamner
Brigham Young Hampton
E. Foster Hampton
Jonathan Hampton
Julia Hampton
Nephi Hampton
Sarah Hampton
Elam M. Hanchett
Mary R. Hanchett
Miranda Hanchett
Nathaniel Hanchett
Alta Hancock
Alvah Hancock
Amy Hancock
Ann Hancock
Charles B. Hancock
Chloe Anna Hancock
Clarissa R. Hancock
Elizabeth Amy Hancock
Francis Marion Hancock
George W. Hancock
Isaac Adams Hancock
Joseph Hancock
Joseph W. Hancock
Levi W. Hancock
Mosiah Hancock
Phoebe Hancock
Solomon Hancock
Thomas Hancock
Charles Harding
Dwight Harding
Eliza Jane Harding
George Harding
Phebe Harding
Alpheus Harmon
Alpheus Harmon Jr.
Appleton Milo Harmon
Jesse P. Harmon
Nehemiah Harmon
Henry Harriman
Isaac Harriman
Dennison Harris
Eleazer Harris
Emer Harris
Fannie Melvina Harris
George W. Harris
Harriet Fox Harris
Joseph Mormon Harris
Margaret Harris
Martin Henderson Harris
Morris Harris
Moses Harris
Ophelia Harris
Silas Harris Jr.
Joseph Hartshorn
Reuben P. Hartwell
John Harvey
Jonathan L. Harvey
Cordelia Haskins
Mary Louisa Haskins
Nathan Haskins
Sarah S. Hastings
Elizabeth Hathaway
James Haun
Elizabeth Haven
Jesse Haven
Maria S. Haven
Calvin Hawk
Rebecca Hannah Hawk
Sarah Hawk
William Hawk
Amos Hawkes
Joseph Bryant Hawkes
Joshua Hawkes
Lucy Hawkes
Nathan Hawkes
Samuel Hawkes
James Hawkins
Sarah Hawkins
Pierce Hawley
Lovina Hay
Thomas Hayes
Anthony Head
Norvil M. Head
James Henderson
Elizabeth M. Hendricks
James Hendricks
Joseph Smith Hendricks
Katherine T. Hendricks
William Dorris Hendricks
Cornelius Hendrickson
Elizabeth Hendrickson
J. P. Hendrickson
James Hendrickson
Lucinda Hendrickson
Margaret Hendrickson
Nicholas Hendrickson
Sophronia Hendrickson
William Hendrickson
Elizabeth Hendrix
Louisa Hendrix
Reuben Hendrix
Samuel Hendrix
Simeon Hendrix
William Hendrix
John P. Herr
Amos P. Herrick
Lemuel Herrick
Lester James Herrick
Lucy Jane Herrick
Samuel Herrick
Henry Herriman
Louisa Herron
Alma Hess
Ann Hess
Elizabeth Hess
Jacob Hess
John W. Hess
Polly Hess
Sarah Hess
Thomas Hess
E. B. Hewitt
Sophia Hewitt
William Hewitt
Joseph Leland Heywood
John A. Hicks
Sylvanus Hicks
Amanda Melvina Higbee
Andrew Jackson Higbee
Chauncey Higbee
DeWitt Higbee
Elias Higbee
Elias K. Higbee
Emma Higbee
Francis M. Higbee
Hannah Higbee
Harriet Higbee
Isaac Higbee
John Mount Higbee
John S. Higbee
Margaret Higbee
Mary Keziah Higbee
Sarah Higbee
Sophia Higbee
Alfred Higgins
Almira Higgins
Nelson Higgins
Nelson David Higgins
Elisha Hill
Eliza Hill
Elizabeth Hill
Isaac Hill
Lucinda Hill
Mary Hill
Nancy M. Hill
Ira Hillman
M. Hillman
Mayhew Hillman
Sarah Hillman
Julia Hills
Arza Erastus Hinckley
Ira N. Hinckley
Jesse Hitchcock
Emily S. Hoagland
Amos F. Hodges
Curtis Hodges
Lucy Hodges
Stephen Hodges
Chandler Holbrook
Diana Eliza Holbrook
Eunice Holbrook
Joseph Holbrook
Joseph Lamoni Holbrook
Mary Mariah Holbrook

Nancy Jane Holbrook
Phebe Holbrook
Sarah Holkins
Thomas W. Hollingshead
David Holman
Ezekiel J. Holman
James A. Holman
James S. Holman
John G. Holman
Joshua S. Holman
Rebecca G. Holman
Sarah Melissa Holman
Jonathan Harriman Holmes
Marietta C. Holmes
Sarah Elizabeth Holmes
Elizabeth Holschaw
Warner Hoopes
Henry James Horne
Joseph Horne
Mary Ann Horne
Mary Isabella Horne
William E. Horner
Alvin Horr
Hannah Diantha Horr
Lorinda Horr
Deborah Houghton
Eli Houghton
Ornan Houghton

John Houston
Abba A. Hovey
Abigail Hovey
Ann Eliza Hovey
Elizabeth W. Hovey
Grafton Wallace Hovey
Joseph Grafton Hovey
Lucy Ann Hovey
Martha Ann Hovey
Orlando Dana Hovey
Richard Howard
Daniel Howe
Fanny Howe
Mary Ann Hoyt

Charles Wesley Hubbard
Emma Hubbard
Mary Ann Hubbard
Anna Maria Hulet
Charles Hulet
Electa F. Hulet
Elizabeth Hulet
Francis Hulet
Jane Hulet
Katherine Hulet
Margaret Ann Hulet
Sally Hulet
Sylvanus C. Hulet
Sylvester Hulet
Hannah Hull
Henry Humphrey
Lamoni Humphrey
Mary Jane Humphrey
Smith Humphrey
Celia M. Hunt
Gilbert Hunt
Harriet Hunt
Hyrum Hunt
Jefferson Hunt
Jefferson Hunt Jr.
John Hunt
Joseph Hunt
Marshall Hunt
Nancy Ann Hunt
Asa B. Hunter
Jesse D. Hunter
Mary B. Hunter
William Hunter
Clark Allen Huntington
Dimick B. Huntington
Fanny A. Huntington
John Dickerson Huntington
Lot E. Huntington
Oliver B. Huntington
P. Huntington
William D. Huntington
Zina Baker Huntington
Catherine Huntsman

Jacob Huntsman
James W. Huntsman
John Huntsman
Lydia Huntsman
Peter Huntsman
Simeon Hurlbutt
James Huston
John Huston
Elias Hutchings
Lucinda Hutchings
Shepherd Hutchings
Charles Walker Hyde
Heman Hyde
Heman T. Hyde
Laura M. Hyde
Martha Ann Hyde
Mary Ann Hyde
Roswell Hyde
William Hyde

I

Julia Ives
Sebe Ives
Elizabeth Caroline Ivie
James Russell Ivie
William S. Ivie
Garret C. Ivins
James Ivins
Mary Ann Ivins
William N. S. Ivins

J

Albert B. Jackman
Amelia Jackman
Levi Jackman
Parimenio Jackman
Amos Jackson
Daniel S. Jackson
Henry Jackson
John Jackson
Henry Jacobs
Henry Bailey Jacobs
Hiram C. Jacobs
Michael Jacobs
Vienna Jacques

Charles Jameson
Julia Ann Jamison
Susanna Jamison
William Jessop
Sally Ann Jewell
Aaron Johnson
Benjamin Johnson
Diadema Johnson
Edward Johnson
Esther Johnson
Ezekiel Johnson
George Washington Johnson
Henry M. Johnson
Huntington Johnson
Jacob Johnson
Jacob H. Johnson
Joseph Ellis Johnson
Lucina Johnson
Mahlon Johnson
Mary Ellen Johnson
Orson Johnson
Jesse W. Johnston
Benjamin Jones
David Jones
James Naylor Jones
Martha P. Jones
Stephen Jones
David Judah
Arza Judd Jr.
Hyrum Judd
Joel Judd
Philo Judd
Zaddock Knapp Judd

K

Elisabeth Keirns
Amanda Ann Kellogg
Ezekiel Kellogg
Hiram Kellogg
Naomi Kellogg
Sophia Kellogg
Adaline Sophia Keller
Alvah Keller
Orin Madison Keller

Roxey Elliott Keller
Charles Kelley
Easton Kelsey
John Averett Kelsey
Polly Z. Kelsey
Joseph Andrew Kelting
Charles Kennedy
Hulda C. Kennedy
James Horace Kennedy
Susan Kent
Lydia Kenyon
Joseph Ketcham
Alma Keys
Eliza Ann Keyes
Susan Elizabeth Keyes
William Henry Keyes
John Killian
Sally Killian
Heber C. Kimball
Heber Parley Kimball
Helen Mar Kimball
Sarah M. Kimball
Vilate Kimball
William Henry Kimball
Caroline M. King
Eleazer King
Eleazer King Jr.
Emily Jane King
Enoch M. King
John M. King
Joseph C. Kingsbury
Eleanor Kingsley
Flora Kingsley
Rachel Kingsley
Adaline Knight
Almira Knight
Anna Knight
Betsy Elizabeth Knight
Elizabeth Knight
Esther Knight
James P. Knight
John Knight
Joseph Knight Jr.
Joseph Knight Sr.
Lydia Knight
Martha M. Knight
Mary Elizabeth Knight
Molly Knight
Nathan K. Knight
Newel Knight
Sally Knight
Samuel Knight
Vinson Knight

L

Mary LaFlesh
Barnabus Lake
Cyrus Lake
Dennis Lake
Eliza Lake
George Lake
Jabez Lake
James Lake Jr.
Jane Lake
Lawrence Lake
Lydia Ann Lake
Sabra Lake
Samantha Lake
Samuel Lake
William Bailey Lake
Abel Lamb
Almira M. Lamb
Brigham Y. Lamb
Edwin R. Lamb
Horace M. Lamb
Joseph S. Lamb
Lisbon Lamb
Sarah S. Lamb
Deborah Lamoreaux
Mary Lampson
Edmond Landon
Johnston F. Lane
Matilda Lane
William W. Lane
Isaac Laney
Edward Larkey
Asahel A. Lathrop
Lois Lathrop
Lydia Lathrop
Lydia Maria Lathrop
David S. Laughlin
John Lawrence
Mary Ellen Lawrence
Rhoda S. Lawrence
John Lawson
William F. Leavens
Cornelia Leavitt
Alonzo LeBaron
Agatha Ann Lee
Alfred Lee
Eli Lee
Elizabeth LaFlesh Lee
Francis Lee
George Henry Lee
Isaac Lee
Jane V. Lee
John D. Lee
P. Lee
Samuel F. Lee
Thomas L. Lee
Deborah L. Leithead
James Leithead
James Lemmon
John Lemmon
Tamer S. Lemmon
Washington Lemmon
Abigail Leonard
Lucy Jane Leonard
Lyman Leonard
Moses C. Leonard
Louisa Leopold
Anna Lewis
David Lewis
Duritha Lewis
James S. Lewis
Joana Lewis
Melinda G. Lewis
Nathan Lewis
Samuel Lewis
Tarleton Lewis
Hannah K. Libbey
Adam Lightner
Lyman O. Littlefield
Mary Thompson Littlefield
Rhoda Littlefield
Sidney John Littlefield
Waldo Littlefield
Julia Ann Lockwood
Almira Henrietta Lott
Alzina Lucinda Lott
Cornelius Peter Lott
Harriet Amanda Lott
John Smyle Lott
Joseph Darrow Lott
Mary Elizabeth Lott
Melissa Lott
Pamelia Jane Lott
James Loveless
John Loveless
Joseph Loveless
Mary Elizabeth Loveless
Nephi Anderson Loveless
Parley Pratt Loveless
Rachel Anderson Loveless
Rachel P. Loveless
Sarah Ellen Loveless
Harriet B. Lowe
Abner Lowry
Elizabeth E. Lowry
George Moroni Lowry
Hyrum Lowry
John Lowry
John Lowry Jr.
Mary A. Lowry
Sarah Jane Lowry
Susan Lucretia Lowry
Amasa Lyman
Asa Lyman
Clarissa Lyman
George Lyman
Louisa Tanner Lyman
Matilda Lyman
Aaron Lyon
Aaron C. Lyon
Windsor P. Lyon
Alma Lytle
Andrew Lytle

Christina Lytle
Hannah H. Lytle
John Lytle
John Milton Lytle
Mary Jane Lytle
Olive Diana Lytle
Syrena Martha Lytle
William P. Lytle

M

John Mabay
Almira Mack
Temperance Mack
Jeremiah Mackley
John Mackley
Ezekiel Maginn
Margaret Mann
Matthew Mansfield
Stephen Markham
Warren Markham
William W. Markham
Ephraim Marks
Rosannah Marks
William Marks
Lucinda Marriott
Molly Marston
Moses Martin
William Martin
Silas Maynard
Duncan McArthur
Elizabeth McAulay
Abigail McBride
Amos McBride
Catherine McBride
Dorcas McBride
George McBride
Isabella McBride
James McBride
Martha McBride
Rebecca McBride
Reuben A. McBride
William McCleary
Christine Stoker McDaniel
John McDaniel
Matilda McDaniel

Zuba McDonald
Susan McKeen
Marcellus McKown
William McLeary
Hannah T. McMeans
James McMillan
Alexander McRae
Eunice McRae
John McVay
Elam Meacham Jr.
Elvira D. Mecham
Martha Mecham
Moses Worthen Mecham
Abigail Meade
Betsy Meade
William R. Melin
Christopher Merkley
Edwin Parker Merriam
Hannah B. Merriam
Thomas Merrill
George Middagh
Charles F. Middleton
Mary Middleton
William Middleton
Garrett W. Mikesell
Hiram W. Mikesell
Independence Mikesell
Jacob Mikesell
John Harrison Mikesell
Mary Glover Mikesell

Ruth C. Mikesell
Elizabeth Milam
Mary Emma Milam
William Milam
Albert Miles
Benjamin F. Miles
Daniel Sanborn Miles
Franklin Miles
Irena Sumner Miles
Joel S. Miles
Margaret Miles
Noah Miles
Rachel Sumner Miles
Samuel Miles

Samuel Miles Jr.
Alma Miller
Clarissa Jane Miller
Clarissa P. Miller
David Arnold Miller
Ebenezer Miller
Elmira Pond Miller
Henry William Miller
Jacob Miller
John Miller
Josiah H. Miller
Susan Hulda Miller
William Miller
Arthur Milliken
Elvira Pamelia Mills
Albert Miner
Matilda Miner
Mormon Miner
Moroni Miner
Tamma Durfee Miner
Benjamin T. Mitchell
Isaac Mitchell
Andrew Moore
Enoch Moore
George Moore
Joseph W. Moore
Melissa R. Moore
George Morey
Cordelia Morley
Diantha Morley
Edith Ann Morley
Isaac Morley
Lucy Diantha Morley
Lucy Gunn Morley
Philena Morley
Theresa A. Morley
Jacob Morris
Arthur Morrison
William Morrison
Moses Morse
Eliza Moses
James Moses
Julian Moses
Margaret Moses
Frederick Mosier
Lucy Ann Munjar

Peter Munjar
William Munjar
Electa Murdock
Eunice Murdock
Gideon Allen Murdock
John Riggs Murdock
Orrice Clapp Murdock
Samuel Murdock
Samuel Musick
Artemisa S. Myers
George Myers
Jacob Myers
John Myers

N

Ruth Naper
Anna Nash
Edmond Nelson
Hannah P. Nelson
Joseph S. Nelson
William G. Nelson
James Newberry
Mary Ann Neyman
Alvin Nichols
Freeman Nickerson
Huldah A. Nickerson
Levi Stillman Nickerson
Uriel Nickerson
William Niswanger
Joseph Bates Noble
Mary B. Noble

O

Almira Oaks
Evan O'Bannion
Harvey Olmsted
Oliver Olney
Gideon Ormsby
Amos Orton
Roger Orton
William R. Orton
David Osborn
Levi Osgood
Patience Osgood
Isaac C. Outerkirk
John Outhouse

Joseph Outhouse
Turner Outhouse
Mahala Overton
Mary Ann Overton
Ephraim Owen
Jedediah Owen
Sally Owen
Caroline A. Owens
James Clark Owens Jr.
James Clark Owens Sr.

P

John Pack
Julia I. Pack
Lucy Amelia Pack
Rufus J. Pack
Ward E. Pack
Henry Packard
Milan Packard
Nephi Packard
Noah Packard
Noah Packard Jr.
Olive M. Packard
Orrin Packard
Sophia Packard
Sophia A. Packard
Jonathan T. Packer
Nephi Packer
Nephi Ewell Packer
Olive Amelia Packer
Ebenezer Page
John E. Page
Rachel Page
Abraham M. Palmer
William M. Palmer
John D. Parker
Mary B. Parker
Mary Jane Parker
Mary (Polly) Parker
Samuel Parker
Thomas B. Parker
Jerusha Parks
Ezra Parrish
Nancy Syrepta Parrish
William R. Parrish

Hannah Parsons
Isaac Parsons
Thorit Parsons
Caroline Partridge
Edward Partridge
Edward Partridge Jr.
Eliza Maria Partridge
Emily Dow Partridge
Lydia Partridge
Archibald Patten
Charles W. Patten
William W. Patten
Jeremiah Patterson
John Pea
Sarah D. Pea
Anna M. Peck
Charity Peck
Electa Peck
Ezekiel Peck
Hannah Peck
Henrietta Peck
Hezekiah Peck
Joseph B. Peck
Martha Long Peck
Martin Horton Peck
Sarah Jane Peck
Thoret Peck
Washington Peck
Lucinda Pendleton
Fredrick M. Penick (Pinnock)
Sarah Perkins
Asahel Perry
Gustavus A. Perry
Hiram Perry
Isaac Perry
Orrin Alonzo Perry
William Perry
Thomas Peterson
David Pettigrew
Elizabeth Pettigrew
Hyrum K. Pettigrew
James P. Pettigrew
Lucy Ann Pettigrew
Albert Petty

John Ralph Petty
William George Petty
Harriet W. Phelps
Henry E. Phelps
Joseph Morris Phelps
Laura C. Phelps
Mary Ann Phelps
Morris C. Phelps
Paulina E. Phelps
William Wine Phelps
June Pickard
Magdalena Pickle
Amanda Heath Pierce
Isaac Washington Pierce
Joseph W. Pierce
Patience Delila Pierce
Nathan Pinkham
Abigail Egglestone Pitkin
George Orrin Pitkin
George W. Pitkin
Alma Porter
Benjamin Porter
Chauncey Porter
Jared Porter
Lyman Wight Porter
Melinda Porter
Nancy Porter
Nathan Tanner Porter
Roxanna Porter
Sanford Porter
Sanford Porter Jr.
Jacob H. Potts
James Powell
Peter Powell
Robert Alonzo Powell
Orson Pratt
Orson Pratt Jr.
Parley P. Pratt
Parley Pratt Jr.
William D. Pratt
Abel Prior
Almira Pulsipher
Charles Pulsipher
Elias Pulsipher

John Pulsipher
Maria Pulsipher
Melana Pulsipher
Polly C. Pulsipher
Sarah Ann Pulsipher
William Z. Pulsipher
Zerah Pulsipher
Jonas Putman

Q

Betsy Quimby

R

Phebe Ramsey
Rachel P. Ramsey
James Randall
Miles Randall
Louisa Cutler Rappleye
Tunis Rappleye
Robert Rathburn
James Rawlins
Jane S. Rawlins
Arthur Morrison Rawson
Caleb L. Rawson
Daniel B. Rawson
Horace S. Rawson
Margaret P. Rawson
Mary Ann Rawson
Samantha Rawson
Sariah Rawson
William C. Rawson
David H. Redfield
George Redfield
Trephena Redfield
William Redfield
John Redford
Calvin Reed
Delia Reed
Elijah Reed
John Reed
Laura Reed
Levi Ward Reed
Rebecca B. Reed
Jane P. Reid
Jesse P. Reid

John Reid
Joseph Reid
William Reid
John Reynolds
Josiah A. Reynolds
Martha M. Reynolds
Mary E. Reynolds
Phoebe R. Reynolds
Sarah Ann Reynolds
Squire Reynolds
Thursa R. Reynolds
Charles C. Rich
Joseph Rich
Sarah Jane Rich
Thomas Rich Sr.
Levi Richards
Ebenezer Richardson
Josiah Richardson
Nancy Richardson
Nancy Rigdon
Phebe Rigdon
Sidney Rigdon
Burr Riggs
Harpin Riggs
John Riggs
Lovina S. Riggs
Nathaniel Riggs
Alanson Ripley
Susan Amelia Risley
Lewis Robbins
Rachel Roberson
Ezekiel Roberts
Angeline E. Robinson
Ann Eliza Robinson
Ebenezer Robinson
George W. Robinson
Sophia Robinson
Horace Rockwell
Luana B. Rockwell
Mary Rockwell
Orin P. Rockwell
Albert Rockwood
Albert Perry Rockwood
Ellen A. Rockwood
Nancy H. Rockwood

Chandler Rogers
David Rogers
David White Rogers
Eda H. Rogers
Elisha H. Rogers
Hannah Caroline Rogers
Henrietta Rogers
Henry C. Rogers
Narcissa Ann Rogers
Nephi Rogers
Noah Rogers
Noble Rogers
Roxanna Rogers
Samuel H. Rogers
Theodore Rogers
Washington B. Rogers
Benjamin W. Rolfe
Elizabeth H. Rolfe
Gilbert H. Rolfe
Horace C. Rolfe
Samuel Jones Rolfe
William Jasper Rolfe
James Henry Rollins
Mary Elizabeth Rollins
Henry Root
Andrew Rose
Ralph Rose
Almedia Sophia Roundy
Jared C. Roundy
Lauren H. Roundy
Lorenzo W. Roundy
Shadrach Roundy
Shadrach Roundy Jr.
Elizabeth Rowe
Jerusha Jane Rowley
William W. Rust

S

Amanda Melvina Sagers
Harrison Sagers
William H. Sagers
Wilkins J. Salisbury
Enoch S. Sanborn
David Walker Sanders
John Franklin Sanders

Joseph Moroni Sanders
Martha B. Sanders
Moses Martin Sanders
Rebecca Ann Sanders
Richard Twiggs Sanders
Mahitabel Sawyer
William Scoby
Elizabeth M. Scott
John Scott
Matilda Scott
David Sessions
David Sessions Jr.
Martha Ann Sessions
Patty Bartlett Sessions
Perrigrine Sessions
Sylvia Porter Sessions
Hannah Seton
John Shaw
Daniel Shearer
Norman B. Shearer
Marcus de Lafayette Shepherd
Roxanna Ray Shepherd
Samuel Shepherd
Almon W. Sherman
Electa E. Sherman
Henry G. Sherwood
Jane Sherwood
Jacob Shumaker
Otis Shumway
Stephen B. Shumway
Eunice B. Shurtliff
Lewis Warren Shurtliff
Luman A. Shurtliff
Lucy Simmons
Caroline K. Skeen
Eleanor S. Skinner
Horace B. Skinner
Angelina Slade
Ann Slade
Benjamin Slade
Clark Slade
Edwin Slade
George W. Slade
O. Slade

Roxanna R. Slade
Albert Sloan
James Sloan
Mary Jane Sloan
Cyrus Smalling
Aaron J. Smith
Abby Jane Smith
Absalom W. Smith
Agnes C. Smith
Albert Smith
Alma Lamoni Smith
Alvira Livonia Smith
Amanda Barnes Smith
Caroline Clara Smith
Catherine Smith
Don Carlos Smith
Elias Smith
Elisha Smith
Elizabeth Smith
Elvira L. Smith
Emma Smith
Esther Victoria Smith
Fanny Smith
Frederick Granger Smith
George Albert Smith
Hortensia Smith
Hyrum Smith
Hyrum Smith Jr.
Jackson Osborne Smith
Jesse Nathaniel Smith
John Smith
John Lyman Smith
Joseph Smith III
Joseph Smith Jr.
Joseph Smith Sr.
Joseph F. Smith
Joshua Smith
Julia Smith
Lucy Smith
Lucy Mack Smith
Lucy Walker Smith
Margaret Smith
Margaret A. Smith
Martha Smith
Mary Fielding Smith

Mary Jane Smith
O. Smith
Samuel Smith
Samuel G. Smith
Samuel H. Bailey Smith
Samuel Harrison Smith
Sarah Smith
Silas Smith
Silas Sanford Smith
Sophronia Smith
Willard Gilbert Smith
William Smith
Abraham O. Smoot
Margaret S. Smoot
William C. Smoot
Harriet E. Snider
Mary Snider
Amanda M. Snow
Elisabeth C. Snow
Eliza Ann Snow
Eliza R. Snow
Erastus Snow
Gardner Snow
James Chauncey Snow
Lorenzo Snow
Mary Snow
Melvina H. Snow
Sarah S. Snow
Willard T. Snow
Zerubabel Snow
John Snyder
Chester Southworth
Sarah Z. Southworth
Andrew J. Squires
Stephen M. St. John
James H. Standing
Clarinda F. Stanton
Constanza C. Stanton
Daniel Stanton
Daniel W. Stanton
Harriet L. Stanton
Melinda E. Stanton
Albert Starr
Almira Starr
Amanda Starr

Amelia Starr
Edward William Starr
Eunice B. Starr
Jane Augusta Starr
Jared Starr
Maryette Starr
Daniel Stephens
George W. Stephens
Henry Stephens
Rebecca K. Stephens
Roswell Stephens Jr.
Roswell Stephens Sr.
Albert Stevens
Edward Stevens
Henry Stevens
Jonathan Edmond Stevens
Lyman Stevens
Marinda T. Stevens
Martha D. Stevens
Reuben Lyman Stevens
Sarah D. Stevens
William Stevens
Edward Stevenson
Elizabeth Stevenson
Benjamin F. Stewart
D. H. Stewart
James William Stewart
John Martin Stewart
Levi Stewart
Lydia Stewart
Malinda Stewart
Nancy Alicia Stewart
Nancy K. Stewart
Nathaniel Stewart
Urban V. Stewart
William J. Stewart
Thirza Stiles
Dexter Stillman
Levi Stiltz
Calvin W. Stoddard
Charles H. Stoddard
Sylvester B. Stoddard
Almira Stoker
Catharine Stoker

David Stoker
Eller Stoker
Jacob Stoker
Jane Stoker
John W. Stoker
Joseph Stoker
Martha Stoker
Michael Stoker
Nancy A. Stoker
Samuel David Stoker
William Stoker
Allen Joseph Stout
Hosea Stout
Samantha P. Stout
Betsy Strait
William Stringham
John Study
Irena Sumner
Jonathan Sumner
Josiah Sumner
Nathan Sumner
Rachel Sumner
Rebecca Swain
Benjamin Sweat
John Sweat

T

Fanny Parks Taggart
Allen Talley
Albert M. Tanner
Allen B. Tanner
David Tanner
Emma Smith Tanner
Freeman Tanner
Helen A. Tanner
James M. Tanner
John Tanner
John Joshua Tanner
Joseph Smith Tanner
Louisa C. Tanner
Lydia Tanner
Lydia Jane Tanner
Mary Louisa Tanner
Myron Tanner
Nathan Tanner

Rachel Smith Tanner
Rebecca Smith Tanner
Sidney Tanner
William Smith Tanner
Allen Taylor
Alma Taylor
Amy Taylor
Eleanor B. Taylor
Elizabeth Taylor
John Taylor
Pleasant Green Taylor
William Riley Taylor
George Bentley Teeples
Huldah C. Teeples
Sidney Teeples
William R. Teeples
John Telford
Eliza Webb Tenney
Emma V. Tenney
William Tenney
Hannah Terry
James Parshall Terry
Joshua Terry
M. Terry
Parshall Terry
Daniel Stillwell Thomas
Henry Thomas
Elizabeth M. Thompson
James Lewis Thompson
James P. Thompson
Julius Thompson
Lewis Thompson
Matilda W. Thompson
Orvil Thompson
Robert B. Thompson
Samuel Thompson
William Thompson
Alice Thornton
Amos G. Thornton
Harriet Thornton
Lydia M. Thornton
Mary Thornton
Oliver Thornton
Thomas Ephraim Thornton

John Thorp
Absalom Tidwell
Sally Tiffany
Abby Jane Tippets
Alvah Tippets
John W. Tippets
Joseph Harrison Tippets
William Plummer Tippets
James Tomlinson
James F. Townsend
Moses Tracy
Truman Tryon
Amos Tubbs
Frances A. Turley
Theodore Turley
Benjamin Turner
Cornelius B. Turner
Nelson Turner
Ann M. Tuttle
Azariah Tuttle
Eleanor Mills Tuttle
Leonard Alexander Tuttle
Luther Terry Tuttle
Daniel Tyler
Samuel D. Tyler

V

Phebe Van Alstine
William Van Ausdall
Keziah Van Benthuysen
Cheney Garrett Van Buren
Lucy Van Buren
Frederick Van Dyke
Joel Vaughn
Elisha Voorhees
George Washington Voorhees

W

John Walker
Lucy Walker
Oliver Walker
William Holmes Walker
Eda Ward
Salmon Warner
Elizabeth Warren
Franklin Watts
R. H. Watts
Edward Weaver
Carolina Owens Webb
Chauncey Gilbert Webb
Chauncey Griswold Webb
Cordelia Amanda Webb
Edward Milo Webb
Eliza Jane Churchill Webb
Martha Ann Webster
Lorenzo Wells
James Wellson
Michael B. Welton
Nathan A. West
Harriet Page Wheeler
John Wheeler
David Whitaker
James Whitaker
Louisa Whitaker
Margaret Whitaker
Nancy Woodland Whitaker
Rosilla Whitaker
Alexander Whitesides
Caroline Whiting
Charles Whiting
Chauncey Whiting
Edith Ann Morley Whiting
Edwin Whiting
Elisha Whiting
Elizabeth T. Whiting
Emeline Whiting
Lovina Whiting
Lovisa Whiting
Sarah Elizabeth Whiting
Andrew Hiram Whitlock
Charles Whitlock
Elizabeth Whitlock
James H. Whitlock
Mary Jane Whitlock
Sally R. Whitlock
Ann Maria Whitney
Caroline Whitney
Horace Kimball Whitney
John Kimball Whitney
Joshua Kimball Whitney
Newel K. Whitney
Orson Kimball Whitney
Samuel Whitney
Sarah Ann Whitney
Alba Whittle
George P. Whittle
Thomas Levi Whittle
Harriet B. Wight
Levi Lamoni Wight
Lyman Wight
Orange Lysander Wight
Wilbur Wightman
William Wightman
Melvin Wilbur
Phoebe Eunice Wilbur
William S. Wilbur
Mary Wilcox
Alexander Wilkins
John G. Wilkins
Nancy K. Wilkins
Sarah Jane Wilkins
Joseph Willard
Jeremiah Willey
Alexander Williams
Almon Williams
Ezra Granger Williams
Frederick Granger Williams
Isabella G. Williams
Lovina Williams
Samuel Williams
Thomas P. Williams
Ira Jones Willis
Margaret Jane Willis
Nancy Ann Wagoner Willis
William Wesley Willis
Aaron Wilson
Almeda Wilson
Bradley Barlow Wilson
Bushrod Washington Wilson
Elijah Wilson
Elvira Wilson
George Clinton Wilson
George Deliverance Wilson
Guy C. Wilson
Henry Hardy Wilson
John Gill Wilson
Lewis Dunbar Wilson
Martha Ann Wilson
Nancy Wilson
Oliver Granger Wilson
Whitford Gill Wilson
Zachariah Davis Wilson
Eliza Jane Wimmer
Lucretia Ann Wimmer
Peter Wimmer
Robert Wimmer
Susan Wimmer
Ada Winchell
Joseph Winchester
Stephen Winchester
Alvin Winegar
John Winegar
Mary Judd Winegar
Samuel Thomas Winegar
William Winget
Dennis Wilson Winn
John Winn
Minor Winn
Nancy Wilson Winn
Alonzo Winters
Hiram Winters
Orson F. Winters
Rebecca B. Winters
Tirzah Winters
Jacob Wirick
Christina Witner
Justin Chauncey Wixom

Sarah Avery Wixom
Solomon Wixon
Daniel Wood
David Wood
Elizabeth Wood
Gideon Durphy Wood
Hannah Daley Wood
Harriet Wood
John Wood
Mary Snyder Wood
Phebe Wood
Rebecca Wood
Sally Wood
Samuel Wood
C. Woodland
John Woodland
John Woodland Jr.
Lucinda Woodland
Polly Woodland
William West Woodland
Wilford Woodruff
Edwin D. Woolley
Franklin Benjamin Woolley
John Woolley Jr.
John Wickersham Woolley
Mary Wickersham Woolley
Rachel Emma Woolley
Samuel Amos Woolley
John Worthen
James Worthington
Rachel Worthington
Asa Wright
Ester Ann Wright
Alexander Wright
*Eveline E. Wright
Joseph Wright

Y

Gad Yale
Aaron M. York
Hannah C. York
Brigham Young
Brigham Young Jr.
Brigham H. Young
Elizabeth Young
Jane B Young
John Young
John R. Young
Joseph Young
Joseph Angell Young
Joseph Bicknell Young
Joseph W. Young
Mary Young
Mary Ann Young
Lorenzo D. Young
Lucy P. Young
Persis G. Young
Phineas Howe Young
Rhoda Young
Seymour B. Young
Vilate Young

Z

Henry Zabriskie
Lewis Zabriskie
Mary K. Zabriskie
William Zabriskie
Catherine Zimmes
Lydia Zimmes
Abraham Zundel
Jacob Zundel